T5-BAL-871

T.

# HOW THEY TRAIN
## Second Edition
## Fred Wilt, editor

# VOLUME I: MIDDLE DISTANCES
## 800 meters/880 yards
## 1500 meters/mile

Publishing history, How They Train:
    First printing, June 1959
    Second printing, January 1960
    Third printing, August 1962
    Fourth printing, December 1965
    Fifth printing, September 1968
    Sixth printing, March 1970

    Second edition, completely revised, in
    three volumes:

    Vol. I:  Middle Distances, March 1973
    Vol. II:  Long Distances, May 1973
    Vol. III:  Sprints and Hurdles, June 1973

Other books by Fred Wilt:
    Run Run Run, 1964
    Illustrated Guide to Olympic Track & Field
        Techniques (with Tom Ecker), 1969
    Mechanics Without Tears, 1970
    International Track and Field Coaching
        Encyclopedia (with Tom Ecker), 1970
    Motivation and Coaching Psychology (with
        Ken Bosen), 1971
    The Jumps: Contemporary Theory, Technique
        and Training, 1972


Library of Congress No.: 73-76247
Standard Book No.: 0-911520-38-4

Printed in the United States of America

# INTRODUCTION TO THE FIRST EDITION

As a 14-year old freshman in a small Indiana high school, I was the only miler on the track team. Track training knowledge was unknown to my coach and others in the area. To better prepare myself for maximum performances, two or three times a week I would train by running a slow two-mile. This was due to the erroneous personal assumption that if I could endure two miles in training, one mile in a race should be easy. But each race was a bitter experience in terms of exhaustion, and I suffered many infuriating defeats at the hands of athletes from larger schools who had the benefit of better coaching and more thorough workout programs. I consulted what literature I could find on the subject of training, but found nothing specific which I could actually use.

In 1940, I enrolled at Indiana University and came under the influence of America's most successful middle distance coach, the late E.C. (Billy) Hayes. Within two months my mile improved from 4:35 to 4:22 and my two-mile from 10:10 to 9:22. Racing which had before meant only pain and exhaustion, now provided me with a feeling of joy in conquering personal fatigue. Hayes taught me the what, how, and why of training as he knew it. By following his advice I was able to achieve results to me previously unimaginable to me.

The coaching success of Billy Hayes was no mere accident. He had a system of training which recognized the individual differences among runners and took into consideration the physiological factors in running. Yet his system was developed primarily through trial and error. He was an Olympic coach in 1936, once toured Scandinavia with an American team, constantly searched for better methods, paid particular attention to the training of others, continually re-examined his own system, and was always willing to change his methods in favor of something better.

Billy Hayes passed away in 1943. Since then, many changes have taken place in training methods generally accepted throughout the world. While the basic principles of training may remain the same, the application of these principles is better understood and applied more universally. This is evidenced by faster performances. Thus in writing this book I have attempted to illustrate the evolution of training methods by describing the actual workout programs of great athletes from 1900 to the present time. Actually, in preparing this book for publication, I have been more of a compiler than a writer, and whenever possible I have let the athletes use their own words in describing their training programs.

The world's first sub-four minute miler, Dr. Roger G. Bannister, has said that "training methods . . . being dependent upon more factors than it is possible at present to analyze, are likely to remain empirical." I wholeheartedly concur, but hasten to add that no empirical training procedure should ever violate known scientific or physiological facts. After a training procedure has been

3

developed through trial and error, it should be possible to justify it on a physiological basis—otherwise it must be subject to question.

You often see items in the press purporting to fabulous workouts by athletes. Much was made of Zatopek having run sixty 440's in a single workout. Yet had he run these 440's in only 85 or 90 seconds it would not have been too much of an accomplishment. It means very little to say the training of an athlete on a specific day involves 10x440 yards. On the other hand, it means very much to say that this workout involved one mile warm-up jogging in eight minutes, followed by 10x440 yards in 62 seconds each, jogging 440 yards in 2½ minutes between each fast quarter, and finally one mile warm-down jogging in 10 minutes. That is why I have attempted to be quite specific in obtaining information on the training of each athlete. To warn youngsters of the grave danger in using the same training as a mature athlete such as Vladimir Kuts or Derek Ibbotson would be rather begging the obvious. This is elementary, and probably something a youngster could not accomplish. I do not recommend that any athlete copy the training procedure of another, but I do maintain that the material herein will suggest many ideas which may be adopted in formulating workout programs suited to an individual runner's needs. Just as no two athletes have identical form, so no two athletes need have the same training program. Literally, as well as figuratively, there is more than one road to Rome. A youngster should not let the herculean training program of the top athletes, as described in this book, discourage him. By using a training program involving gradual adaption to stress over a prolonged period of time, workouts consisting of both quality and quantity may be accomplished. However, intensive training absolutely does not insure successful racing. The training merely makes successful racing possible. A runner must also have the all-important factor of mental attitude, a will to win, a subconscious desire for victory, courage, tenacity, and a competitive "killer instinct" in order to achieve racing success.

My own twenty years of competitive racing have been a beneficial experience in many ways. Through the sport of track I have enjoyed many pleasant associations which probably would not have been otherwise available to me. It is probably thus fitting that I should attempt to make some tangible contribution to the sport in token of appreciation. My attempted contribution is an effort to disseminate empirical (not scientific) training knowledge.

I would like to thank the athletes and contributors who have made the presentation of this material possible. Special thanks go to Hal Higdon for the illustrations; to Bert and Cordner Nelson of "Track & Field News" for their obvious labor of love in publishing this; and to my beloved wife, Eleanor Hebsgaard Christensen, for doing so much (more than I like to admit) of the work involved.

Fred Wilt    July, 1959

# PREFACE TO THIS EDITION

The first edition of HOW THEY TRAIN, originally printed in 1959, listed more than 150 runners and their training patterns, half mile to six miles and up. The popularity and value of this book was such that we thought a new edition, with some of the current top athletes, was clearly called for. We have been collecting material and sending out questionnaires for a number of years now. In fact, so much valuable material was obtained that it was decided to split HOW THEY TRAIN—II into three volumes. Thus, three separate books are now available: HOW THEY TRAIN—MIDDLE DISTANCES, HOW THEY TRAIN—LONG DISTANCES; and HOW THEY TRAIN—SPRINTING AND HURDLING. The last volume covers an area not previously handled and fills a need in the track community, we believe.

We are also reprinting some useful material from the first edition. The original introduction (above) is included as it indicates how a book on training programs should be approached by a beginning or veteran runner. Further, so that the very interesting (and still useful) training routines of some of the great athletes of the past would not pass into oblivion when the first edition of HTT went out of print, some of these entries are being reprinted. Thus, the training of Herb Elliott, John Landy, Emil Zatopek, Kuts, Hägg, Nurmi, Harbig, and others is reproduced in this second edition, and provides very interesting comparisons with the training of today's champions.

Data on present-day athletes were obtained over a period of time, thus only a few will offer 1971 or 1972 training schedules. Steve Prefontaine and Dave Wottle, for instance, contributed their information in 1969, and their training then may have little relation to their build-ups for the 1972 Olympic Games. But both were good runners in 1969, and certainly their training for that year contains lessons and much of interest to any coach and runner.

Each entry lists the name of the athlete, his club or school, and his age and year when the training details were obtained. Also given in most cases are personal statistics (birth date, height and weight, when the athlete began running, etc.). And most entries divide the training year by seasons and end by giving details of strategy, personal philosophy, career history, etc., updated where necessary.

Not every runner in these pages is of world class caliber, but all are fairly well known, at least in the USA. This gives a mix of training programs of top-flight runners and lesser lights, which should be of value. Some classifications were arbitrary, e.g. Fanie Van Zyl is equally proficient in the 800 and 1500/mile, but was put into the mile section, as was Michel Jazy, who could have easily fit into the book on longer distance training. Others of course like Ralph Doubell and Peter Scott were 800/880 specialists and there is no doubt about their classification.

We'd once again like to express our sincere thanks to the athletes who shared their training ideas and procedures with us, and to the authors and publications who assisted in making available material included in this edition. Also, thanks to the following individuals for their kind efforts in assisting with the writing of profiles contained herein: Gary Childs, Bill Blewett, John T. Goegel, Alexander W. Saltmarsh, Don Kopriva, Joey Haines, Robert Hoffenberg, Larry J. Myers, Robert Henson, Ken Stone, Bill Huyck, Mark Green, John Boyd Scott, Larry Main, H. David Dunsky, Stuart Warner and Dr. Gordon N. Schafer.

# ILLUSTRATIONS/PHOTO CREDITS

# CONTENTS

# Fred Wilt

# A LOGICAL BASIS FOR THE TRAINING OF RUNNERS

It is sometimes assumed that so-called modern methods of training are of recent origin. In truth, much of what runners do today in preparation for competition was common practice among the Greeks more than 2,000 years ago. However, the athletes of old did not have the benefit of scientific justification for their training routines as we do in many cases today.

Because slaves performed whatever work was to be done during that era, free citizen-athletes of Greece were at liberty to use all of their time for training and competition. This is precisely what was done by top-class performers among the ancient Greeks. Thus, any question in the moral domain arising from total devotion of an athlete's time to training had its roots in antiquity. As an example of this alleged excessive concentration on athletics to the exclusion of perhaps more important aspects of life today, one US candidate for the 10,000-meter race in the 1972 Olympics has been reliably reported to repeat the following workout as many days each week as he can tolerate: run continuously at a pace of 6 to 7 min/mile for 7 to 8 miles at 10:00 AM and also at 2:00 PM, and 10 miles in the late evening, for a total of approximately 50 miles of running per day.

Regardless of their event of specialty, ancient Greek athletes sought first to develop a firm foundation of general physical fitness by running, walking, jumping, wrestling, games, calisthenics and weight lifting, before progressing to workouts more specifically related to their competitive specialties. By the same token, athletes today seek first to develop a "hard core" of basic fitness (general endurance, muscular endurance, strength, and power) prior to undergoing specialized training for their racing events.

The specialized training for running used by the ancient Greeks included the "anatrochasmos" (running backward), "peritrochamos" (running in circles), "ekplethrizin" (running forward and backward over a few meters distance, lessening this each time to zero length), running in sand, running on hard surfaces, hopping, jogging, skipping, and running with large hoops which they rolled in front of them, especially during warming up. They were empirically aware of the "overload principle" (which specifies that increases in endurance and muscular strength result from an increase in intensity of work performed in a given unit of time) and the principle of gradual adaptation to stress (Milo of Croton lifted and carried a calf daily from birth to maturity as a means of progressive resistance exercise).

The Hellenic runners trained all day to a strict four-day uninterrupted cycle known as "Tetras." The first day was preparation or easy training, consisting of a number of short, brisk exercises designed to motivate the athlete in anticipation for the next day's efforts. The second day was concentration, involving hard, all-out effort, leaving the athlete in a state of extreme fatigue. The third day was relaxation, during which the athlete recovered by only very light training or rest. This sequence ended with the fourth day, moderation, which was devoted to moderate training (Wilt, 1972).

Modern-day competitive racing distances may be generally described as sprints (up to and including 440 yards or 400 meters), middle distances (880 yards or 800 meters to and including 6 miles or 10,000 meters), and long distances (all races beyond 10,000 meters, and including the marathon, which is 26 miles, 385 yards or 42,195 meters). The 440 yards race might be described as an endurance sprint, while the middle distances may properly be divided into short-middle distances (880 yards to 2-miles) and long-middle distances (3-miles to 6-miles). It is important that these distances be clearly identified when selecting the type of training to be used if optimum physical preparation for competition is to be achieved.

## BASIC TRAINING TERMINOLOGY

**Training,** the series of physical activities executed for the purpose of increasing efficiency in running and racing, should be a continuum throughout an athletic lifetime. The specific physical fitness that permits an athlete to run a given distance in a faster time is acquired most efficiently through use of carefully planned training which is tailored to the length and anticipated speed of the racing distance. In order to identify the factors involved in our discussion of training, organize the material presented, and establish precision of meaning for the purpose of this chapter, certain terminology is reviewed hereafter in ultra-simplified form.

Each **workout,** the physical activities which occur during one session of training, should be preceded by a warm-up and followed by a warm-down. The **warm-up** refers to the preliminary exercise used as physical and mental preparation for strenuous exertion which is to follow immediately, and the warm-down is simply exercise gradually diminishing in intensity following severe exertion, for the purpose of facilitating return of the circulatory system and bodily functions to a pre-exercise state. The same warm-up is often used prior to training and to competition. A useful warm-up for all racing distances is one mile of continuous running, at a speed of three minutes for the first 440 yards, 2½ minutes for the second, two minutes for the third, and alternately sprinting 50 yards and jogging 50 yards throughout the final 440 yards. This should be followed by five minutes of calisthenics, after which the athlete is ready to go directly into the training session. The same warm-up prior to competition may be followed by ten minutes of rest before going directly into the race. The usual warm-down is merely 880 yards to one mile of jogging.

**Jogging** refers to running at a speed of two to three minutes per 440 yards, or eight to twelve minutes per mile.

**Sprinting** means running at maximum speed. Cadence in good sprinting is 4½ (occasionally five) strides per second. It requires about 45 steps to run a 100 yards sprint race. Stride length, indicating the distance covered with one step, varies in length between seven feet (84 inches) and 8½ feet (102 inches) in sprinting. By contrast, stride length in middle distance running varies between five feet (60 inches) and six feet (72 inches). In sprinting, both feet are off the ground about 60% of the time, while in middle distance running the body is out of contact with the ground about 50% of the time.

**Striding** indicates any running speed between jogging and sprinting.

From a training viewpoint, **recovery** implies restitution, restoration, or return to a relatively normal resting state following exercise.

**Stress** indicates any condition which places an unusual burden on the organism. It may be regarded as rate of wear and tear, or simply anything of which an individual experiences too much. Stress may be any infectious, painful, adverse, or deleterious force or various abnormal state that tends to disturb the body's normal physiologic equilibrium (homeostasis).

**Fatigue,** by common usage, indicates a sensation of tiredness or a psychic state. It is a condition in which the performance of a certain amount of work meets with increased difficulties and is carried out with a decreasing effect. There is a subjective feeling of locomotor inhibition which eventually leads to complete muscular impotence. Biochemically, it indicates the accumulation of lactic acid in the muscles to the extent of seriously impeding muscular contractility.

**Metabolism** is the term applied generally to all chemical reactions which occur in living cells. However, it is often confined to oxidations which are the ultimate source of biological energy.

**Aerobic** means "with oxygen." Aerobic metabolism occurs in muscles when there is available an adequate supply of oxygen, and results in complete utilization of the carbohydrate to produce carbon dioxide and heat.

**Anaerobic,** the opposite of aerobic, means "without oxygen." Anaerobic (without oxygen) metabolism may occur when there is an inadequate supply of oxygen. The performance of physical exercise where the oxygen cost per minute exceeds the oxygen intake is known as anaerobic work. During severe exercise, oxygen intake is inadequate to supply the oxygen requirement for production of the energy demanded, and the energy for muscular contraction is derived anaerobically from a complex series of chemical reactions. This liberation of energy in the absence of oxygen is an anaerobic chemical reaction. During the course of this complex reaction, lactic acid $(C_3H_{603})$ and other non-volatile acids are formed as the end product of anaerobic metabolism of glucose of glycogen. Lactic acid adversely affects muscular activity. An accumulation of more than a few tenths of one percent in the blood results in muscular pain and contraction of the muscles ceases. Although lactic acid must eventually be oxidized, buffers in the blood (collectively known as the alkaline reserve) can neutralize great quantities of lactic acid during exercise. There is a limit to the amount of lactic acid each individual is willing to tolerate before decreasing his work rate or ceasing the activity.

For a variable period of time after exercise, this anaerobically produced accumulation of lactic acid demands oxygen for oxidation. During the post-exercise period, the "oxygen-debt" is paid in terms of oxygen intake for oxidation of the lactic acid accumulated during exercise. **Oxygen debt** is the difference between oxygen requirement during exercise and oxygen intake during the performance of the exercise **(oxygen requirement minus oxygen intake)**. It is the amount of oxygen required during the post exercise recovery period to reverse the anaerobic reactions of the exercise period.

The **overload principle** specifies that increases in muscular strength and endurance result from an increase in intensity of work performed in a given unit of time.

**Endurance** is the ability to withstand fatigue, or the ability of the body to withstand the stresses set up by a prolonged activity. It implies a considerable range of meaning generally related to prolonged activity which produces fatigue. (Fatigue indicates a sensation of tiredness or a psychic state. Biochemically, it indicates the accumulation of lactic acid and other non-volatile acids in the muscles to the extent of seriously impeding muscular contractility.)

**Endurance** includes aerobic endurance (general endurance), anaerobic endurance, and muscular endurance (which may be subdivided into aerobic muscular endurance and anaerobic muscular endurance). These types of endurance are closely related within the unity of the human organism. The effectiveness of each to some extent is dependent upon the others. The identification and development of the various types of endurance become important in accordance with the competitive racing distance for which the athlete seeks to prepare himself. In terms of running a given distance in the fastest possible time, it would be most ineffective for the sprinter to concentrate primarily on the development of aerobic endurance, or for the long distance runner to concentrate mainly on the development of anaerobic endurance.

**Aerobic endurance,** also known as general endurance or stamina, is the general ability to withstand fatigue of the entire organism in the presence of a sufficient supply of oxygen over a prolonged period. It involves the ability to resist fatigue under conditions where oxygen intake and oxygen requirement for the activity are kept at a steady and equal level. This quality, sometimes called cardio-vascular endurance, and circulo-respiratory endurance, is most evident in work of medium intensity involving the entire organism (Nett, 1965).

**Anaerobic endurance** is endurance in the absence of oxygen. It is the general ability to withstand fatigue of the entire organism when oxygen is in insufficient supply. In running, this type of endurance is of special importance in the short-middle distance events. Anaerobic endurance may be termed speed-endurance (Nett, 1965).

**Muscular endurance** is local endurance which may be either aerobic or anaerobic. Aerobic muscular endurance is the ability of the muscles to withstand fatigue of the locally active muscle groups in the presence of a

12

sufficient oxygen supply, or oxygen endurance of the locally active muscles. Anaerobic muscular endurance is the ability to withstand fatigue in locally active muscles or muscle groups in the absence of an adequate supply of oxygen, or local muscular endurance under conditions of oxygen deprivation. Extent of the blood supply in the muscles involved, oxygen transport at the tissue level, muscle tissue viscosity, and strength are among the qualities upon which muscular endurance is dependent (Nett, 1965).

A well-trained athlete can absorb approximately six liters of oxygen per minute during severe exercise, and can tolerate a total oxygen debt of approximately 15 to 20 liters.

**Weight training** is simply the lifting of weights to develop strength. Numerous repetitions of lifting light weights appears to develop endurance in the muscles involved, while the lifting of progressively heavier weights, necessitating fewer repetitions, develops greater strength. Essential features of weight training for strength development are lifting heavy weights, using a near maximum number of repetitions of which the athlete is capable at the moment, and the gradual increase of the poundage lifted as strength of the athlete increases. The most recent recommendations for weight training by runners in all racing events by Russian and German authorities appear to be light weights and high numbers of repetitions. Weight training for runners might be opposed on grounds that it could increase body weight. The best advice on this issue is to include heavy weight lifting as part of the runner's training, but discontinue it when and if a significant increase in body weight is noted.

## SELECTED METHODS OF TRAINING

### 1.  Sprint Training

Sprint training involves the repetition of short sprints as a means of preparation for competitive running. Since sprinting means running at absolute maximum speed, there can be no such phenomenon as an "easy sprint." The faster the running speed, the longer the stride. A runner therefore takes his longest stride when sprinting. When starting from a static position, it requires about six seconds to accelerate to maximum speed. Sprinters should therefore run at least 60 yds. on each sprint, so as to produce the experience of moving at maximum speed. Top sprint speed is about 36 ft. per second. The maximum strength exertion required in sprinting will cause the heart to beat in excess of 200 beats per minute. At this rate the heart does not fill maximally during diastole. For this reason, a heart-expansion stimulus apparently does not occur during sprinting. Sprint training therefore does not produce an increased stroke volume of the heart, although it strongly stimulates metabolism in the muscles. Thus sprinters have relatively small hearts, hardly different from the hearts of non-athletes. Because sprinting muscles contract with great speed against high resistance, they become thicker, faster, and stronger. The effect of sprinting as a means of training is the development of speed and muscular strength.

## 2. Continuous Slow-Running Training

Continuous slow-running training refers to running long distances at relatively low speeds. The distances covered in this type of training should be related to the racing event. For example, a miler might run three to five times his racing distance or more. A three-miler might run six to twelve miles, and the six-miler might run 12 to 18 miles continuously at slow speeds. The heart beats approximately 150 beats per minute during this type of training, and the speed depends upon the ability of the athlete (Nett, 1960a). For example, eight minutes per mile or 120 seconds per 440 yds. might be sufficiently fast for a relatively inexperienced high school miler, while six minutes per mile or 90 seconds per 440 yds. might be the appropriate speed for an international class 5000 meters runner to bring the heart-rate to 150 beats per minute. This type of training has maximum effect in terms of producing aerobic endurance. It is the superior method of increasing the stroke-volume of the heart, capillarization of the musculature, and facilitation of the circulatory ability of the organism. This training represents the first step in gradually adapting to withstand fatigue. It is not limited to any particular racing distance, and forms the basis upon which later to apply faster training more nearly related to the specific racing speed and distance. This type of training should not be timed, and for psychological reasons it is usually done on cross-country or golf courses or roads, but may take place on the running track.

## 3. Continuous Fast-Running Training

Continuous fast-running training differs from slow continuous running in terms of speed. Because the pace is faster, fatigue is encountered sooner. The distances covered are often in excess of racing distances, but not usually so long as those used in slow, continuous running. An 880 yds. runner might run ¾ mile to 1½ miles, and repeat the distance one to four times, recovering by alternately walking and jogging five minutes after each run. A six miler might run eight to ten miles at a steady, fast, continuous pace, or perhaps run four to five miles on two or three occasions, alternately walking and jogging for five minutes after each during one workout. Although varying with individual differences, the pace is sufficiently fast to cause the heart to beat well in excess of 150 times per minute, perhaps approaching 180 beats per minute during the latter stages of the distance covered. This training develops aerobic endurance. It represents a more intense form of effort than slow, continuous running, and seeks gradually to condition the organism to tolerating the stresses encountered in running at faster and faster speeds.

## 4. Interval Training

Interval training (interval running) is a form of training for competitive running involving a formal pattern of alternately running fast and slow. Briefly, it is fast-slow running. Five variables are found in interval training: the **distance** of the fast runs, the **interval** of rest or recovery between fast runs, the number of **repetitions** of the fast run, the

**time** of the fast run, and the type of activity during the recovery or rest between fast runs. Note that the first four of these variables can be remembered by the code word—D-I-R-T. The fifth variable, activity between fast runs, is usually either walking or jogging. Interval training involves repeatedly running a specific distance at predetermined speed, resting a specific interval following each fast run, recovering through use of a specific activity (walking or jogging) during the interval between fast runs. This type of training usually takes place on the track, with the fast runs being carefully timed with stopwatch. However, this need not always be the case, and in areas where winds are high and snow covers the the ground a major portion of winter, carefully clothed athletes can be seen doing interval training workouts on the roads with the wind at their backs, recovering while returning by jogging to the starting point against the wind, often without the benefit of stopwatch timing. The quality of work is much higher in interval running than in continuous running. Both 10x110 yds. in 14 seconds, with 110 yds. recovery jogging after each, and 10x660 yds. in 2:00 minutes, with 220 yds. recovery jogging after each, would be examples of interval training. However, their effects would be entirely different in terms of which develops aerobic endurance and which benefits anaerobic endurance. For this reason, a careful distinction should be made between slow and fast interval training.

5. **Slow Interval Training**

Slow interval training is thought to develop aerobic endurance. The speed is faster than in continuous fast-running training, thus adapting the athlete to running at a more intense effort. In this type of formal fast-slow running, the heart beats at the rate of approximately 180 beats per minute during the "effort" or fast phase. Slow interval training is usually confined to distances up to 880 yds. These include repetitions of 110, 220, 440, and 880 yds. The speed of the effort phase may be empirically determined in the following ways:

a)      Add four or more seconds to the athlete's best 110 yards time with a running start. As an example, if the athlete's best 110 yards is 12 seconds, his time for repetitions of 110 yds. in slow interval training should be 12 plus 4 equals 16 seconds. For this athlete 20 to 40x100 yds. in 16 to 20 seconds, jogging 110 yds. in 45 seconds after each fast 110 yds. would be a slow interval training workout. This workout might take the form of 2 to 4 x (10x110 yds., jog 110 yds. after each fast 110. Walk two to four minutes after each series of 10x110).

b)      Add six or more seconds to the athlete's best 220 yds. with a running start. For example, if the athlete's best 220 yds. is 26 seconds, his time for repetitions of 220 yds. would be 26 plus 6 equals 32 seconds. For this athlete, 10 to 20x220 yds. in 32 to 36 seconds, jogging 220 yds. in 90 seconds after each fast 220 yds. would be a slow interval training workout.

c)      Ascertain the best average speed an athlete can maintain for 440 yds. in the middle distance race in which he expects to compete, and add four or more seconds. As an example, a six-miler whose best mark is 30:00 minutes will average 75 seconds per 440 yards. Thus his 440 yards pace for slow interval training might be 75 plus 4 equals 79 seconds (or even slower if he so desires). For this athlete, an example of a slow interval training workout might be 4 to 5 x (10x440 yards in 80 seconds each, jogging 110 to 220 yards after each. Walk three to five minutes after each set of 10x440 yards).

A 9:20 ability two-miler averages 70 seconds per 440 yards. His pace in slow interval training would be 70 plus 4 equals 74 (or possibly slower) seconds per 440 yards. For this athlete, 3x (10x440 yards in 74 seconds, jog 220 yards in 90 seconds after each. Walk five minutes after each set of 10x440) would represent a slow interval training workout.

A 4:12 ability miler averages 63 seconds per 440 yards in this race. His 440 yard pace in slow interval training would be 63 plus 4 equals 67 (or more) seconds. For this miler, 3 x (5x440 yards in 67 seconds, jog 220 yards in 90 seconds after each. Walk five minutes after each set of 5x440) would represent a slow interval training workout.

A 1:48 ability half-miler would average 54 seconds per 440 yards. His 440 yards pace in slow interval training would be 54 plus 4 equals 58 or more seconds. For this 880 yards runner, 3 x (3x440 yards in 58 to 60 seconds, jog 440 yards after each. Walk five minutes after each set of 3x440) would represent a slow interval-training workout.

6. **Fast Interval Training**

Fast interval training is thought to develop anaerobic endurance or "speed-endurance." It is used after a background of aerobic or general endurance has been established. The heart should beat in excess of 180 beats per minute during the "effort" or fast phase in this type of interval training. It develops the ability of the runner to withstand fatigue in the absence of an adequate oxygen supply. Although it has not been proved that fast interval training increases the alkaline reserve, the result is nevertheless an apparent increased ability of the organism to tolerate the acid products of fatigue. As a practical matter, experienced runners have empirically discovered this training develops a "specific" endurance necessary to run a given middle distance race at a faster pace. Fast interval training is considerably more intense in terms of speed than continuous slow-running, continuous fast-running, or slow interval training, and therefore results in a more powerful stimulus to muscle metabolism. It is ordinarily confined to repetitions of 110, 220, and 440 yards, although this need not be the case.

The speed during the effort phase of fast interval training may be empirically determined in the following ways:

a)      For 110 yard repetitions, add 1½ to 2½ seconds to the athlete's best time for that distance with a running start. If an athlete's best 110 yards is 12 seconds, his time for repetitions of this distance in fast interval training would be 12 plus 1½ to 2½ equals 13½ to 14½ seconds. For this athlete, 2 to 3 x (10x110 yards in 13½ to 14½ seconds, jog 110 to 220 yards after each. Walk three to five minutes after each set of 5x220 yards.) would represent a fast interval training workout.

b)	For 220 yard repetitions, add three to five seconds to the athlete's best time for that distance using a running start. If an athlete's best 220 yards is 25.0 seconds, his time for repetitions of this distance would be 25 plus 3 to 5 equals 28 to 30 seconds. For this athlete, 3 to 5x(5x220 yards in 28 to 30 seconds, jog 220 yards after each. Walk three to five minutes after each set of 5x220 yards.) would represent a fast interval training workout.

c)	For 440 yard repetitions, ascertain the best average speed an athlete can maintain for 440 yards in the middle distance race in which he expects to compete. Subtract one to four seconds from this figure. If an athlete's best mile time is 4:40 (averaging 70 seconds per 440 yards), his time for repetitions of 440 yards might be 70 minus 1 to 4 equals 66 to 69 seconds. A 4:00 minute miler (averaging 60 seconds per 440 yards) might subtract one to four from 60 and run repetitions of 440 yards in 56 to 59 seconds during fast interval training. For the four minute miler, such workouts as 2 x (5x440 yards in 58-59 seconds, jog 440 yards after each. Walk five minutes after each set of 5x440 yards); 3x440 yards in 57 seconds, jog 440 yards after each, walk five minutes after each set of 3x440; and 5x (2x440 in 56 seconds, jog 440 yards after each. Walk two to four minutes after each set of 2x440), would be examples of fast interval training.

d)	Because the pace is slower in longer middle distance races, the length of training repetitions may be extended to cover 880 yards during fast interval training for athletes competing at these distances. In this case, the speed is determined merely by subtracting four seconds from the average pace the athlete can maintain for 880 yards over the full longer middle distance event. For example, the 15:00 minute three miler and 30:00 minute six-miler will average 2:30 per 880 yards. For these athletes, the pace for repetitions of 880 yards would be 2:30 minus 4 equals 2:26. A workout of 6 to 12x880 yards in 2:26, jog 440 to 880 yards after each, would represent fast interval training for such athletes.

In the case of longer middle distance runners, it has not been positively established whether more thorough adaptation to running stress results from fast interval training repetitions of 880 yards, or the use of this and longer training distances performed as repetition running (described hereafter). Short middle distance performers usually prefer repetitions of 880 yards and longer distances in the form of repetition running.

7.	**Repetition Running**
Repetition running differs from interval training in terms of the length of the fast run and the degree of recovery following each fast effort. It involves repetitions of comparatively longer distances with relatively complete recovery (usually by walking) after each. Interval training includes repetitions of shorter distances (ordinarily 110 to 440 yards) with less than complete recovery after each by jogging a distance equal to the fast run in a time period two to three times as long as required to complete the fast run. Repetition running is usually concerned with repetitions of distances such as 880 yards to two miles with relatively complete recovery between, during which time the heart rate reduces well below 120 beats per minute. Such repetitions at reasonably fast pace in

accordance with individual competitive objectives over distances approximating the athlete's competitive event tend to duplicate the duration of stress encountered under racing conditions. The speed in this type of training determines whether a training benefit accrues in terms of aerobic or anaerobic endurance. Repetitions at a pace considerably slower than racing speed tend to develop aerobic endurance. At a pace approaching racing speed, repetition running appears more likely to enhance anaerobic endurance. Repetitions of running beyond racing distance should be significantly slower than racing speed. When repetition running reaches racing speed, the length of the fast runs should not exceed half the competitive distance for which the athlete is training. Because of the higher speed involved, repetition running tends to be more exhausting than continuous slow running training, continuous fast running training and slow interval training.

It would be unwise to specify rigid training times in repetition running due to the role played by individual differences among athletes. However, the following suggestions may serve as a rough guide in terms of speed when using this type of training:

a)      The half-miler may run 2 to 4 x 660 yards at average racing plus two to three seconds for the 660 yards or 1 to 3 x ¾ mile at average racing pace plus ten seconds per 440 yards. Thus a two-minute half-miler, averaging 60 seconds per 440 yards or 1:30 for 660 yards in competition, might run 2 to 4 x 660 yards in 1:32 to 1:33 during one workout. A 1:54 half-miler, averaging 57 seconds per 440 yards in competition, might run 1 to 3 x ¾ mile in 57 plus 10 equals 67 seconds per 440 yards or 3:21 each.

b)      A miler may run 2 to 4x¾ mile in average racing pace plus three to four seconds per 440 yards, or 1 to 3x¼ mile at average racing pace plus five to six seconds per 440 yards. Thus a 4:16 miler, averaging 64 seconds per 440 yards, might run 2 to 4x¾ mile in 64 plus 3 to 4 equals 68 seconds per 440 yards, or 3:21 to 3:24. A 4:20 miler, averaging 65 seconds per 440 yards, might run 1 to 3x¼ mile in 65 plus 5 to 6 equals 70 to 71 seconds per 440 yards, or 5:50 to 5:55.

c)      A two-miler might run 4 to 6x¾, 3 to 4x1 mile, 2 to 4x1¼ mile, or 2 to 3x½ mile at a pace of average racing speed plus three seconds per 440 yards.

d)      A three-miler might run 5 to 8x¾ mile, 4 to 6x1 mile, or 2 to 4x1½ mile at average racing speed plus three seconds per 440 yards. He might also use repetition running workouts such as 2 to 4 x two-miles at average racing speed plus five seconds per 440 yards.

e)      A six-miler might run 8 to 10x¾ mile, 6 to 8 x 1 mile, 5 to 8x1¼ mile, or 4 to 5x1½ mile at average racing speed plus three seconds per 440 yards. He might also use repetition running workouts such as 3 to 5 x 2 miles, 2 to 3x3 miles, or 1 to 2x4 or 5 miles at average racing speed plus five seconds per 440 yards.

## 8.    Speed-Play or Fartlek

Speed-play is a form of training featuring informal fast-slow running, as opposed to the formal fast-slow running found in interval training. It means running at alternate fast-slow pace, preferably (though not necessarily) over natural surfaces such as golf courses, grass, or woods, with a basic emphasis on

18

fast running. Fast and slow interval running, repetition running, sprinting, walking, and continuous fast running training are informally combined in speed-play training over unmarked surfaces not unlike the cross-country course. This psychologically stimulating form of training, when properly executed, should develop both aerobic and anaerobic endurance, in addition to muscular hypertrophy. Speed-play training, formerly known as "fartlek" (a Swedish word meaning speed-play) when originally developed in Sweden during the 1930's, has the disadvantage of lack of control by the coach. Unless the athlete is alert, responsible, conscientious, and devoid of laziness, speed-play training is apt to degenerate to nothing more than a long, slow jog in the country, thus depriving the runner of most of the training benefits which accrue when this form of training is properly executed (Wilt, 1959).

The various forms of training previously described may be combined in almost innumerable ways as speed-play training. The following is an example of one speed-play workout which might be used by an experienced miler. The distances and speeds specified are approximate:

a) Jog ten minutes as a warm-up.

b) Five minutes brisk calisthenics.

c) 1 to 2x¾ to 1¼ mile at a fast, steady pace which might be described as ¾ full speed. Walk five minutes after each.

d) 4 to 6x150 yards acceleration sprints (jog 50 yards, stride 50 yards, and sprint 50 yards. Walk 50 yards after each).

e) 4 to 6x440 yards at slightly faster than racing effort. Jog 440 yards after each.

f) Walk ten minutes,

g) Two miles continuous slow run.

h) Walk five minutes

i) 8 to 12 x 110 yards at 1½ to 2½ seconds slower than best effort, jogging. 110 yards after each. Walk five minutes.

j) 4 to 6x60 yards sprints uphill. Walk back after each.

k) Jog one mile as a warm-down.


9. **Interval Sprinting**

Interval sprinting is a method of training whereby an athlete alternately sprints 50 yards and jogs 60 yards for distances up to three miles. In this type of training, the athlete sprints 4x50 yards per 440 yards, jogging 60 yards after each. This training is believed to develop aerobic endurance.

After the first few sprints, fatigue tends to inhibit the athlete from running at his absolute top sprint speed. Similarly, fatigue causes the athlete to slow his recovering jogging to a speed perhaps as slow as walking. For this reason, the training effect of interval sprints is quite unlike that of sheer sprinting followed by adequate recovery (Berbin, 1965).

10. **Acceleration Sprinting**

Acceleration sprinting is the gradual acceleration from jogging to striding, followed by sprinting. For example, an athlete may do repetitions of jog 50 yards, stride 50 yards, and sprint 50 yards, followed by walking 50 yards and repeating. Other examples of acceleration sprints include jog 60, sprint 60, and walk 60 yards; and jog 110, stride 110, sprint 110, and walk 110 yards. It is important that the athlete walk for recovery after each acceleration sprint, so as to be sufficiently recovered to run a maximum speed during the next effort. This type of training primarily develops speed and strength. Acceleration sprints are especially valuable when sprinting outdoors in cold weather, since the athlete gradually reaches top speed and thereby avoids the risk of muscle injury which might occur when suddenly reaching top speed in low atmospheric temperatures.

TABLE 1

| TYPE OF TRAINING | SPEED | DEVELOPMENT BY PERCENTAGE | |
| | | AEROBIC ENDURANCE (General Endurance) | ANAEROBIC ENDURANCE (Speed-Endurance or Specific-Endurance) |
|---|---|---|---|
| Repetitions of sprints | 90% | 4% | 6% |
| Continuous slow-running | 2% | 93% | 5% |
| Continuous fast-running | 2% | 90% | 8% |
| Slow-interval | 10% | 60% | 30% |
| Fast-interval | 30% | 20% | 50% |
| Repetition running | 10% | 40% | 50% |
| Speed-play | 20% | 40% | 40% |
| Interval sprinting | 20% | 70% | 10% |
| Acceleration sprinting | 90% | 5% | 5% |
| Hollow sprints | 85% | 5% | 10% |

11. **Hollow Sprints**

Hollow sprints are two sprints, joined by a "hollow" period of recovery jogging. Examples include sprint 50, jog 50, sprint 50, and walk 50 yards for recovery prior to the next repetition; sprint 110, jog 110, sprint 110, and walk 110 yards before the next repetition; and sprint 220, jog 220, sprint 220, and walk 220 yards before repeating. If sufficient recovery occurs during the walking following each hollow sprint, this type of training should develop muscular strength and speed.

20

It seems logical to suspect that each of these types of training has at least some effect upon speed, aerobic endurance, and anaerobic endurance. Nevertheless, it is known that greater training benefits, in these factors, follow from some forms of training than others. Table 1 illustrates the approximate percentage of development in each of these factors possibly resulting from various types of training. It is admitted unhesitatingly that these figures result from the empirical observations of the author, although they are based to some extent upon recent research findings (Roskamm, et al, 1962).

## TABLE 2

Oxygen requirement according to racing distances.

| EVENT | TOTAL $O_2$ REQUIREMENT | OXYGEN UPTAKE | OXYGEN DEBT |
|---|---|---|---|
| Marathon in 2 hours, 15 minutes | 763.0 liters, equals 100% | 745.0 liters, equals 97.5% | 18.0 liters, equals 2.5% |
| 10,000 meters in 29:00 minutes | 178.0 liters equals 100% | 160.0 liters, equals 90% | 18.0 liters, equals 10% |
| 5,000 meters | 90 liters, equals 100% | 72 liters, equals 80% | 18 liters, equals 20% |
| 2 miles in 9:00 minutes | 40 liters, equals 100% | 22 liters equals 55% | 18 liters, equals 45% |
| 1,500 meters in 3:40 | 38.0 liters, equals 100% | 20 liters, equals 52.5% | 18 liters, equals 47.5% |
| 800 meters in 1:45 | 27.6 liters, equals 100% | 9.6 liters, equals 35.0% | 18.0 liters equals 65.0% |
| 800 meters in 2:00 | 27.0 liters, equals 100% | 9.0 liters, equals 33.33% | 18.0 liters 66.66% |
| 400 meters in 45.0 seconds | 22.1 liters, equals 100% | 4.1 liters, equals 18.5% | 18.0 liters, equals 81.5% |
| 200 meters | 20.0 liters, equals 100% | 1 to 2 liters equals 5 to 10% | 18 to 19 liters equals 90 to 95% |
| 100 meters | 8 to 10 liters equals 100% | 0.0 liters, equals 0.0% | 8 to 10 liters equals 100% |

### Recovery During Training

Recommendations for the duration of recovery between fast training runs and the nature of activity during such recovery are made on an empirical basis.

In middle distance training at repetitions of running which cause the heart to beat approximately 180 times per minute, recovery need be no more than walking until the heart slows to two-thirds this rate, or 120 beats per minute (20 beats in ten seconds), before starting the next repetition. When recovery is by walking, runners may check their heart-rate after fast repetitions by placing one hand directly over the heart and counting the beat for ten seconds, on a stopwatch. Simply multiply the ten-second count by six for the rate per minute (Wilt, 1964).

If the recovery is by jogging, the athlete is usually advised to jog a distance equal to that of the preceding fast run in a time period equal to two to three times the number of seconds required to negotiate the fast run. This, however, is subject to certain refinements, as the speed used during the fast run will influence the duration of recovery jogging.

As an athlete improves in physical condition and ability, recovery jogging during slow interval training may be gradually reduced. For example, superior athletes might jog only 110 yards after slow intervals of 220 and 440 yards, even though athletes of lesser ability might require a full 440 yards jog for recovery.

During fast interval training, the speed of the fast efforts is of sufficient intensity to justify recovery by jogging a distance equal to that of the fast run, and sometimes a longer distance. As an example, a runner using fast repetitions of 110 yards might jog 220 yards for recovery after each.

In both slow and fast interval training, recoveries are intentionally kept incomplete so as to start each repetition with a degree of fatigue products in the blood and muscles. The recovery should be sufficiently long to allow the next repetition to be run at the same speed as the previous effort, but a longer recovery should be avoided if optimum training benefit is to result.

One objective of training may be to accustom and adapt the athlete to running with a high heart-rate over a prolonged distance (preferably at least the duration of the anticipated racing distance). It may be possible to contribute to this goal by faster jogging during the recovery phase in fast interval training. It is now known that the heart beats well in excess of 180 beats per minute during the course of competitive middle-distance events. It has also been observed that during recovery jogging (at speeds of two to three minutes per 440 yards) in interval training, the heart seldom reduces to a rate below 160 beats per minute. By increasing the speed of recovery jogging from two-three minutes per 440 yards to approximately 80 seconds per 440 yards, the heart-rate will remain in the vicinity of 180 beats per minute during the recovery phase of interval training.

Examples of workouts using this recovery jogging speed for the purpose of sustaining a high heart-rate might be as follows:

(a) 6 to 20x110 yards in 12-14 seconds each. Jog 330 yards in 60 seconds after each.

(b) 4 to 12x220 yards in 28-30 seconds each. Jog 220 yards in 40 seconds after each.

(c)  3 to 6x330 yards in 42-45 seconds each. Jog 550 yards in 1:40 after each.

When using such recovery to sustain a high heart-rate during fast interval training, the speed of the effort phase must be quite high for the purpose of elevating the heart-rate well over 180 beats per minute.

The use of such fast recovery jogging (approximately 80 seconds per 440 yards) by necessity drastically increases the severity of the training. Therefore, such training should be reserved for experienced athletes, and even then it should be used judiciously and only intermittently.

At the present time most superior middle distance runners recover during interval training by jogging. It is unknown as to whether jogging or walking is preferable or more desirable from a training viewpoint in either slow or fast interval training. One minute of walking usually results in as much or more recovery as two minutes of jogging, on the basis of decrease in heart-beat. In jogging, contact is broken with the ground and there is a period of "double float" wherein both feet are off the ground during the course of each step, thus the energy requirement is higher than for recovery walking. Since jogging requires more energy than walking and is therefore more fatiguing, it is generally assumed that jogging has a more beneficial training effect. The physical motions used in jogging have little, if any, more relationship to the movements used in running at racing speed than do the movements used in walking. It might be argued that a greater number of fast repetitions could be run within a given workout during the time saved by walking for recovery, thus producing a more beneficial total training effect. Because the heart seldom beats slower than 160 beats per minute during recovery jogging, it may be argued that aerobic endurance is developed in this way.

During fast continuous running training, repetitions of ¾-mile, 1-mile, 1¼-mile, etc., may be followed by recovery walking until the heart rate slows to 120 beats per minute.

Walking is recommended for recovery during repetition running. The high speed and longer distances used in this type of training demand that the recovery be more complete than in slow and fast interval training. The heart may be permitted to reduce in rate well below 120 beats per minute during recovery walking, so as to permit the next repetition to be run at the desired speed.

As in repetition running, walking is also recommended for recovery between repetitions of sprinting. If recovery is insufficient, then what might be intended for sprinting becomes slower than maximum speed, and the net training effect is quite different from that expected of sprint training, namely the development of sheer speed.

### Training Volume

The total volume of training, exclusive of warm-up, warm-down, and recovery walking and jogging, which an athlete may reasonably use in a single workout in an effort to achieve optimum training benefit must be determined with due regard to numerous factors, not the least of which is individual differences. Youth and novices are advised to err on the side of too little rather than too much running in the beginning and early stages of their training. More experienced athletes in reasonable physical condition usually have no need to fear too much running, and indeed one of the problems in the past has been failure to use enough total running volume to achieve best competitive results. A total of ten to 20 sprints with walk recovery following each is not unreasonable during one workout for the sprinter. Middle distance runners may cover 1½ to two times racing distance during a fast interval training workout. For example, a miler might run 12 to 16x220 yards, jog 220 yards, after each, during a fast interval training workout. The middle distance runner may cover a total of two to three times racing distance during the course of a slow interval training session. For example, a two miler might run 16 to 24x440 yards during slow interval training. Olympic and world-record caliber runners frequently far exceed the above training volumes, but there is always a question as to the point of diminishing returns in excessive training volumes. This question cannot be answered on the basis of present knowledge (Wilt, 1964).

### Training Emphasis According to Racing Distances

From Table 2, it is apparent that after an athlete has undergone a basic conditioning period and acquired a foundation of general endurance which has produced gradual adaptation of the entire organism to the stresses of running, his training during the speeding-up period for competition, and during the actual racing season might logically receive specific training emphasis in accordance with the speed, aerobic and anaerobic requirements of his racing distance. It is the opinion of this author that in the case of the middle and long distance runner, regardless of the aerobic and anaerobic requirements of his race, he should include at least some sprinting during most training sessions. Table 3, reflecting the author's personal recommendations, may serve as a rough guide to the percentage of speed, aerobic, and anaerobic training to utilize.

### Annual Training Plan

When utilized as a continiuum throughout an athletic career, training may be divided on a yearly basis into the basic conditioning period, speeding-up period, racing season, and the season of active rest. These four periods are different in length, do not sharply change from one to another, and should tend to overlap as the training is gradually intensified.

The period of active rest immediately follows the racing season. Rest is only relative during this period. General physical condition is maintained through games and activities such as basketball and swimming. Some running may be done, but the training load should be considerably reduced. The level of physical condition previously achieved should not be permitted to completely deteriorate, thus active rest rather than complete rest is recommended. This period should occupy approximately four weeks.

The basic conditioning period is used to develop aerobic endurance and strength, while gradually adapting the organism to tolerating increasingly more intense efforts of running. This phase may occupy three months, with the fourth month gradually overlapping the first month of the speeding-up period.

During the speeding-up phase, major emphasis is placed upon the development of speed and anaerobic endurance. The first month of this phase overlaps the fourth month of basic conditioning, while the fourth month of speeding-up

TABLE 3

Recommendations for training emphasis according to racing distances.

| EVENT | SPEED | AEROBIC ENDURANCE (General endurance) | ANAEROBIC ENDURANCE (Speed-endurance or specific endurance) |
|---|---|---|---|
| Marathon | 5% | 90% | 5% |
| Six miles | 5% | 80% | 15% |
| Three miles | 10% | 70% | 20% |
| Two miles | 20% | 40% | 40% |
| One mile | 20% | 25% | 55% |
| 880 yards | 30% | 5% | 65% |
| 440 yards | 80% | 5% | 15% |
| 220 yards | 95% | 3% | 2% |
| 100 yards | 95% | 2% | 3% |

overlaps the first month of the racing season. The principle of progressive loading is evident here, as the overload principle is used in applying training efforts more intense in terms of speed and greater volume (distance) than can be anticipated during actual competition. The repetitions of running are faster than racing speed (though by necessity much shorter than racing distance), and their total when added is far in excess of the actual competitive objective.

The first month of the racing season overlaps the fourth month of the speeding-up period, and may cover approximately five months. Training is adjusted to maintain and increase previously developed aerobic and anaerobic endurance and speed, while simultaneously introducing sufficient rest to permit best competitive efforts. Longer recovery periods prior to competition may be recommended, and the total number of workouts per week may be reduced. The more severe workouts are taken a reasonable number of days prior to competition, and in some cases the intensity of training may be curtailed. A certain volume and speed of training, depending upon individual differences, must nevertheless be maintained during racing season, as it is well known that insufficient training, even when racing frequently, can result in an athlete losing his previously acquired preparation for fast competitive efforts.

Although running is among the oldest of competitive sports, its history in terms of measurement is relatively short. The attempted application of scientific knowledge to training is an even more recent development, and has a parallel not unlike the history of scientific thought.

Table 4 will serve to illustrate the approximate duration of training phases on a yearly basis.

## TABLE 4
### Annual Training Plan

| TYPE OF TRAINING | MONTHS | TRAINING PERIODS |
|---|---|---|
| Aerobic endurance and strength | 1 2 3 4 | Basic conditioning |
| Anaerobic endurance and speed | 5 6 7 | Speeding-up |
| Maintain and increase previously acquired speed and aerobic and anaerobic endurance. Introduce **sufficient rest and produce** best competitive efforts. | 8 9 10 11 | Racing |
| Informal general physical activity | 12 | Active Rest |

The ancient practitioners of the pseudo-science of alchemy sought to transform the base metals into silver and gold. Thanks to the efforts of research and scientific thought, we now know the futility of this endeavor. This is not to say that alchemy has vanished, as the hope of great wealth through conversion of cheap materials into precious metals did not die easily.

In a sense, the training advocated by coaches in the past has often resembled the alchemists' search for the philosopher's stone, alias world records. Gradually the application of scientific knowledge has been introduced, and modern coaches now tend to seek a scientific foundation upon which to base their methods. Nevertheless, it is still possible to hear of training methods promising magic results being advocated with reckless disregard for scientific fact.

This superficial survey of training for running is much less than all-inclusive. The problems of how far, how fast, and how often to run in training for optimum competitive results still remain largely unsolved. Progressive coaches today are by no means comfortable and secure in their knowledge of training details. There can be no doubt that considerably more physiological research in a number of directions is needed if the art of training is to be placed on a more scientific basis.

## BIBLIOGRAPHY

Berben, Dieter, (1965). "Uber die Intervallsprints", *Die Lehre der Leitchtathletik,* No. 40, page 1231.

Donath, Rolf, (1969). *Mittelstrecken and Hindernislauf.* Berlin: Sportverlag Berlin.

Jarver, Jess, (1964). *The How and Why of Physical Conditioning for Sport.* Adelaide: Rigby Limited.

Morgan, R.E., and Adamson, G.T. (1961). *Circuit Training.* London: G. Bell and Sons Ltd., second edition.

Nett, Toni, (1959a). "Zur Lehre des Lauftrainings", *Die Lehre der Leichtathletik,* No. 46, page 1091.

Nett, Toni, (1959b). "Zum Sprinttraining", *Die Lehre der Leichtathletik,* No. 47, page 1115.

Nett, Toni (1959c), "Tempolauf-Training/Muskel-Stoffwechsel-Training", *Die Lehre der Leichtathletik,* December 22, 1959, No. 49, page 1221.

Nett, Toni, (1960a). "Dauerlauftraining", *Die Lehre der Leichtathletik,* No. 2, page 35.

Nett, Toni, (1960b). *Der Lauf.* Berlin: Verlag Bartels and Wernitz, pages 36-38.

Nett, Toni, (1965). "Die Haupt-Trainingsprinzipien Intervall und Dauerprinzip", *Die Lehre der Leichtathletik,* No. 34, page 1023.

Nett, Toni, (1956). "Physiological Considerations of Pace in Running Middle Distance Races", *International Track and Field Digest,* page 219.

Roskamm, H., Reindell, H., and Keul, J. (1963). "Physiologische Grundlagen der Trainings-methoden". *Die Lehre der Leitchtathletik,* No. 28, page 635.

Roskamm, H., Reindell, H., and Keul, J. (1962). "Physiologische Grundlagen der Trainings-methoden", *Die Lehre der Leichtathletik,* No. 28, page 659.

Wilt, Fred (1959). *How They Train.* Los Altos: Track and Field News.

Wilt, Fred (1964). *Run Run Run.* Los Altos: Track and Field News.

Wilt, Fred (1972). "Conditioning of Runners for Championship Competition", *Journal of The American Medical Association,* August 28, 1972, Vol. 221, No. 9, page 1017.

# HOW THEY TRAIN
## 800m./880 yards

# Markku Aalto

MARKKU KALERVO AALTO, Helsinki Kisa-Veikot. Age 20, 1969.

BEST MARKS: I 1,000m., 2:36; 800m., 1:48.5; 600m., 1:19 (lap time on way to 800m); 400m., 48.2; 200m., 22.0; 100m., 10.9.

PERSONAL STATISTICS: Born March 25, 1949 at Helsinki, Finland. Started racing in 1964 at age 15.

PRE-RACE WARM-UP: About 4 kilometers in 50 minutes. First, jog 1 kilometer, then 5 minutes calisthenics, then 2 kilo. jog, then 5-10 minutes calisthenics, then 2-4 x 100 meter sprints (first about 15 seconds, and then faster, last about 11.5). Followed by 1 kilometer jog in woods or on grass.

PRE-TRAINING WARM-UP: 2 kilometers in 30 minutes. First 2 kilo. jog, calisthenics, 2 x 100m; the first in 14 seconds, the 2nd in 12 seconds, in woods or grass.

FALL CROSS-COUNTRY TRAINING: Monday through Saturday: Long distance jog of 16 kilometers (roughly 10 miles) on roads, 4 minutes per kilometer. Sunday: Rest. (Distances of jog may vary, but total distance is 100 kilometers per week.

WINTER TRAINING: Same as above, except one day a week, 7 x 300m in 45 seconds with a 5-8 minute recovery. Total distance per week is about 80 kilometers.

SPRING/SUMMER TRACK SEASON: Monday—PM (5:00), 5x100m. 10 minutes walk recovery between each. Tuesday—PM (5:00), Long jog of about 10 kilometers in woods, with break for calisthenics, and walking. 5 minutes per kilometer. Wednesday—PM (5:00), 3x150m. 12 seconds each, with 10 minute interval.Thursday—PM (5:00), Jog 7 kilometers in woods at speed of 5 minutes per kilo. After 2 kilos. of continuous running, 2-4x150m. sprints in 12 seconds (walk back recovery). Friday—Same as above or 3x90m. (in the middle of sprint, 30 meters as fast as I can run). Walk back recovery. 5 minutes rest, then 2x150 meters. Saturday—Rest. Sunday—Competition.

Participates in 10 outdoor, 2 indoor races annually. Rests one day before competition. Does not use orthodox weight training, but does do a type of resistance work, running 3x14m., while another runner holds one end of springs that are attached around his waist. Competes 5-6 hours after last meal.

Holder of 8 Finnish junior championships. Finnish record for 400 meters. Winner of 2 senior indoor championships, 4-time member of teams that competed with other countries. Holder of Northern countries junior record for 800 meters. Senior outdoor 800 meter champion.

STRATEGY: "I have tried hard to seek stiff competition, so I have not needed to lead. I prefer to follow and win by sprinting on the finish."

## Wade Bell

CHARLES WADE BELL, University of Oregon and Oregon Track Club. Age 24,1969.

BEST MARKS: 2-miles, 9:04.6; mile, 3:59.8; ¾-mile, 2:56.7; 1000m., 2:18.7; 1000y, 2:06.7; 880y, 1:46.1; 800m, 1:45.0; 660y, 1:18.7; 440y, 48.3; 330y, 34.9; 220y, 21.6; 100y, 10.1.

PERSONAL STATISTICS: Born January 3, 1945 at Ogden, Utah. 5'11", 156 lbs. Started racing in 1960 at age 15.

PRE-RACE WARM-UP: 2-mile jog in 14-16 minutes. 4x110y easy strides in 16-17 seconds. 5-10 minutes of calisthenics. 2x100y in 13-15 seconds with walk between.

PRE-TRAINING WARM-UP: Same as pre-race warm-up.

FALL TRAINING: Monday: 4x440y in 58-60 seconds with 440y jog interval; 4x(660y, 440y, 330y, 220y, 110y) in 1:42-1:45, 66-68 seconds, 45-48 seconds, 28-30 seconds, and 13-15 seconds with full distance recovery jog; 4-6-mile jog at 6-8 minutes per mile. Tuesday: 5-7-mile jog at 6-8 minutes per mile. Wednesday: 6-8x330y in 42-45 seconds. 8-10 mile run at varied pace. Thursday: 5-7-mile slow, easy run. Friday: 10-12-mile run at even pace: 4-6x165y in 22-25 seconds. Saturday: 3-5-mile easy jog; 4-6x110y in 16-18 seconds. Sunday: mile time trial at 66 seconds per 440y pace; 7-mile run.

WINTER TRAINING: Monday: 6x165y in 20 seconds with 110y jog interval; 11x165y in 22 seconds with 110y jog-walk interval; 4-6 mile easy run. Tuesday: 5-7-mile run at 6-8 minutes per mile; 4x110y in 16-18 seconds. Wednesday: 440y, 660y, 440y, 220y in 60 seconds, 1:30, 60 seconds, and 26 seconds with full rest; 4-6x220y in 27 seconds; 2x(660y, 440y, 330y,

220y, 110y) in 1:45, 68 seconds, 48 seconds, 30 seconds, and 14 seconds. 4-6-mile run. Thursday: 5-7-mile jog. Friday: 1-2x165y in 19.5-20.5 seconds; 3-mile jog. Saturday: Race. Sunday: Long run of 10-15 miles.

SPRING/SUMMER TRAINING: Monday: 4x440y in 57-59 seconds; 4x220y in 25-26 seconds; 1x(660y, 440y, 330y, 220y, 110y) in 1:45, 68, 48, 30, and 14 seconds; 4-mile jog. Tuesday: 4-6x165y in 19.5-20.5 seconds on grass; 5-mile run at 6-8 minutes per mile. Wednesday: 660y, 440y, 660y in 1:28, 58 seconds, and 1:28 with full recovery; 4x220y in 25-26 seconds; 4x110 in 11.5-12.5 seconds; 5-mile run at 6-8 minute pace. Thursday: 4-6-mile run, 6-8 minute pace. Friday: 1-2x165y in 19-20 seconds. 1-3-mile jog on grass. Saturday: Race. Sunday: 10-mile easy run.

Bell did two workouts per day, year around. The morning workouts at 7 a.m. consisted of a 2-4-mile run at a pace of 7-9 minutes per mile. On Tuesday or Thursday mornings he often did 5x(4x110y) increasing in speed from 22 to 14 seconds. He jogged 1-3 miles on mornings before races. A rest of 3 weeks to 3 months followed both his spring racing and fall training seasons.

In 1967 Bell won the NCAA, AAU, and Pan American Games, and he set collegiate records in the 880y (1:46.1) and 800m (1:45.0). In '68 he again won the AAU and gained a berth on the Olympic team. He was coached by Bill Bowerman and Charles Hislop. He ran 4-6 indoor, 6-8 outdoor, and 2 cross-country races per year.

Wade Bell

John Boulter

# John Boulter

JOHN PETER BOULTER, Bolton United Harriers and Achilles Club. Age 23, 1963.

BEST MARKS: 3-mile, 14:03; mile, 4:01.3; 1500m, 3:43.3; 880y, 1:47.8; 440y, 48.3(r).

PERSONAL STATISTICS: Born November 18, 1940 in Colchester, England. 6'1", 161 lbs. Started racing in 1957 at age 17.

WINTER TRAINING: Lifts weights 3 or 4 times a week. Most training is done cross-country, rarely more than 10 miles. Also uses fartlek and interval training, but not on the track.

SPRING/SUMMER TRAINING: Monday: 4x440 in 58 with 1 minute recovery. Rest 6 minutes. Repeat. Rest 6 more minutes. Repeat. Tuesday: 4x15 minutes sprint fartlek up hills. Wednesday: 8x220y, starting at 30, increasing to 26, with 75 seconds recovery. Rest 15 recovery. 6x50y sprint. Friday: Rest. Saturday: Race. Sunday: Easy workout, often a run in the country.

Lifts weights 3 or 4 times a week during the winter.

Coached by Lionel Pugh. Likes to have a race of some sort every week, but not more often than once every three weeks for big meets. Training sessions are usually 90 minutes to 2 hours.

Canadian mile champ in 1961. Equalled United Kingdom record in 880y with 1:47.8 in 1963.

*John Boulter has been a world class middle distance runner since the early sixties. In 1967 he was ranked fourth in the world in the 800/880, winning the AAA and world Games titles. His best 800m. mark came in 1966, 1:46.5, and in 1969 he ran a 3:59.2 mile.*


# Dicky Broberg

ERIK (DICKY) BROBERG, Worcester, Defence, Stellenbosch U. Age 20, 1969.

BEST MARKS: 400: 46.5 seconds; 800: 1:46.4. Trains 5/6 days out of season 4/5 in season.

PERSONAL STATISTICS: Born July 8, 1949, Worcester, South Africa. 5'10½", 160 lbs.

PRE-TRAINING WARM-UP: Exercise and sprints.

PRE-RACE WARM-UP: Exercise and sprints.

WINTER TRAINING: Monday: 1-1½ hour run and exercises. Tuesday: 1-1½ hours fartlek and exercises. Wednesday: Half hour hill running: hour fartlek. Thursday: 1-1½ hour fartlek and exercises. Friday: 1 hour run and exercises. Saturday: Competition or 1 hour fartlek. Sunday: Rest.

SUMMER TRAINING: Monday: 4x600 meters. Tuesday: 4x440 meters; 6x400m, 6x200m. Wednesday: 12x200m; 3x100m. Thursday: 6x200m; 6x100m. Friday: 6x100m; 6x50m. Saturday: Competition or same as on Wednesday. Sunday: Rest.

ANNUAL PROGRESSION: 1966: under 17: 880 1:53.2; 1966: Under 19: 880 1:50.4. 1967: 400m. 48.2. 1968: 400m. 46.7, 800m 1:47.8. 1969: 400m. 46.5: 800m 1:46.4.

Coached by John Broberg (father). Likes to compete.

*Dicky Broberg returned the fifth best 800m. time in history in 1971, 1:44.7, and was ranked fourth in the world that year. He also had a 46.3 400m. In 1970, he ranked 8th in the 800 with a best of 1:45.9.*

## Chris Carter

CHRISTOPHER SYDNEY CARTER, Hove Athletic Club, England. 6 ft. ½ in. tall, 176 lbs. 1965.

BEST MARKS: Mile, 4:10.6; 800m, 1:46.6, 600m, 1:17.5; 440y, 49.0; 220y, 22.6.

PRE-RACE WARM-UP: 15-20 minutes easy jogging; 10 minutes stretching exercises; 2-4x60-80m striding in spikes.

PRE-TRAINING WARM-UP: Same as pre-race warmup.

WINTER TRAINING (Feb. 1965): Monday: 11-mile road run in 65 minutes. Tuesday: Weight training of bench presses, squats or cleans, curls, and military presses. Wednesday: 6 miles crosscountry in 34 minutes. Thursday: 1 hour fartlek on golf course; weight training. Friday: 9-mile road run in 55 minutes or rest if race scheduled Sat. Saturday: Easy jogging for about 2 hours. Sunday: 6x440y in 60-62 seconds with 2 minute interval; 4x150 fast strides on track.

SUMMER TRAINING (Sept. 1965): Monday: 800m race in 1:50.1. Tuesday—AM, 4x440y in 53 seconds with 5 minute interval. PM, 6x220y in 23.5-24.5 seconds with 220y jog recovery. Wednesday: Long slow warm-up; 14x150 in 15.5-16.0 seconds with 150y walk recovery; 4x60y sprint starts. Friday: Easy jogging and 6x150y very fast with walk back recovery. Saturday: Rest. Sunday: 800m race in 1:46.6.

Carter is coached by John Le Masurier. He trains with weights from October until April, usually twice per week. He normally runs 5 or 6 days per week, doing 7 to 8 workouts per week.

*Chris Carter again ranked tenth in the world in 1966. His 1:46.3 gave him fourth in the European Championships. That year, he also had a fifth in the Commonwealth Games.*

Chris Carter                    Pat Collins

# Pat Collins

PATRICK JOSEPH COLLINS, Oregon State University, Corvallis, Oregon. Age 20, 1968.

BEST MARKS: 2 mile, 10:18; mile, 4:24; 1000, 2:11; 880, 1:48.4; 660, 1:20; 440, :48.2; 330, :34.6; 220, :21.9; 120HH, :15.0; 100, :10.1.

PERSONAL STATISTICS: Born December 5, 1948 at San Diego, California. 6'4", 173 lbs. Started racing in 1956 at age 8.

PRE-RACE WARM-UP: Lots of stretching, then a mile jog concentrating on looseness. Then about 5 quick sprints of around 100 yards each. Rest ten minutes, shake out and run.

PRE-TRAINING WARM-UP: Mostly jogging and stretching to build up concentration and get ready to work.

FALL CROSS-COUNTRY TRAINING: During the first part of the week runs 7-12 miles at 6:00 pace and later in the week runs 8x330 in :45 or 8x440 in :60, followed by a two-mile run. Runs cross country meets, but does not take them seriously.

WINTER TRAINING: Monday: 7 or more miles at 6:00 pace. Tuesday: Some 220's at :25 and 2x330 in :40. Wednesday: 3 timed (1:21 or near that) 660's. Thursday: 3 sets of 440 in :65, 330 in :45, 220 in :26 and striding a 165. Friday: Jog, shake out and stretch. Saturday: Meet. Sunday: Quick 3 mile morning run, relax and study.

SPRING/SUMMER TRACK RACING SEASON: Monday: Easy morning jog of 2-3 miles. Afternoon training of 3 sets of 440 in :65, 330 in :45 and stride 165. Stride 10 fast 110's. Tuesday: 4-5 miles at 6:00 pace on road. Stride 3x220 (in :27) and 5x110. Wednesday: 3 timed 660's (1:20-1:25) with quick (:54-:55) first 440, and with 1 lap walk-jog between. Rest 5:00 and stride 5x110. Thursday: Morning jog of 2 miles. 6 miles at 6:00 pace in afternoon. 4-5 starts from blocks. Friday: 3 miles of Fartlek. Saturday: Race. Sunday: 3 miles at 6:00-7:00 pace in afternoon.

DURATION OF WORKOUTS: 2 hours beginning at 2:30 PM.

Participates in cross country races, 4 indoor meets and 8-12 outdoor meets. Does no weight training. Coached by Bernie Wagner, Mike Keller, Edward Bader, Chuck McNeil and Jim Puckett. Oregon high school 880 champ in '66, '67. Won '69 Kennedy Games.

STRATEGY: In high school liked to lead; in college prefers to hold back and kick last 200 yards.

In 1970, Pat Collins was rated 9th in the world. His 1:46.5 placed second in the NCAA 880.

Tom Courtney

# Tom Courtney

THOMAS WILLIAM COURTNEY, Fordham University and New York A.C. Age 25, 1958.

BEST MARKS: Mile, 4:07; ¾ mile, 2:56; 1000m, 2:19.3, 1000, 2:08.6; 880, 1:46.8 (world record); 800m, 1:45.8; 600, 1:09.5 (world record); 400m, 45.8; 220, 21; 100, 9.7.

PERSONAL STATISTICS: Born August 17, 1933 at Newark, New Jersey. 6'2", 183 lbs. Started racing in 1949 at age 16.

PRE-RACE WARM-UP: Jog 1 mile. 4x80-110 at near sprint speed. Walk 110 yards after each. Jog 10 minutes.

PRE-TRAINING WARM-UP: "Very little unless I am going to sprint hard right off the bat. I do not believe that about 2 miles of easy pick-ups is the best warm-up."

MID PRE-COMPETITIVE SEASON TRAINING: Monday: 10x300 in 36. Walk 300 after each. Tuesday: 6x880 in 2:10. Walk 440 after each. Wednesday: 10x300 in 36. Walk 300 after each. Thursday: Light sprints. Acceleration sprints and sprints on grass. Jog 3-4 miles. Friday: 10x300 in 36. Walk 300 after each.

"As I get closer to racing season I reduce the number of fast runs and run them faster. My work is on the track and usually not with a watch—only because I have no coach."

MID COMPETITIVE SEASON TRAINING: Monday: 4x300 in 32. Walk 300's. "My fastest 300 in this set of 4 is 29.8." Tuesday: ¾ mile in 3:00 (60, 65, 55). "I have run ¾ mile in 58, 60, 58 for 2:56, and in 60, 68, 52 for 3:00." Walk 10 minutes. 2x300 in 33. Walk 300's. Wednesday: 3x300 in 31-32. Walk 300's. "Sometimes I run 660 yards in 1:18 for pace." Thursday: Rest. Friday: Jog 1 mile. 3x80, fast. Jog 80 after each. Saturday: Race. Sunday: Rest.

Duration of workouts: 1½ hours, starting at 3:00 PM.

Runs 20 indoor and 10 outdoor races each year in USA. Also runs approximately 20 races on AAU tours abroad during summer. Pre-competitive training period covers 4 months. Coached by Joe McCluskey, Dean Cromwell (while in Army), Arthur O'Connor (4 years), and Emil Piel. Virtually self-coached since graduation from Fordham. Very little weight training, but feels it would help runners. Courtney was the 1956 Olympic 800m. champion.

STRATEGY: "Having a good knowledge of each opponent's best races, I usually figure out how each will run in the championship races. I figure out my

pace accordingly and make it even, but fast enough to beat my opponents
to the tape.''

Tom Courtney

## Bill Crothers

WILLIAM FREDERICK CROTHERS, Univ. of Toronto and East York Track Club. Age 28, 1968.

BEST MARKS: 1 mile, 4:02.4; ¾ mile, 2:57; 1000m., 2:18.9; 1000y, 2:06 (t); 800m., 1:45.6; 880, 1:46.8; 660, 1:18 (t); 440, 46.2; 300m., 34.2 (t); 200m., 21.7; 220, 21.8; 100y, 10.2.

PERSONAL STATISTICS: Born December 24, 1940 at Markham, Ontario, Canada. 6'0'', 155 lbs. Started racing in 1956 at age 15.

PRE-RACE WARM-UP: 3 miles in 40 minutes; easy jogging for 4 laps or so. Then walk and jog and visit washroom for 5-10 minutes. Few stretching exercises. Run 4-6 110's, building up to 12 second speed. Walk or jog until race.

PRE-TRAINING WARM-UP: 1-1½ miles. Jog 4-6 laps on grass. Run 4-5x110's at 12 to 14 seconds. Sometimes a few flexibility exercises.

FALL CROSS-COUNTRY TRAINING: Monday: Run 5-8 miles on road. Tuesday: 6x880 at 2:35-2:22 on track. Wednesday: Run 4-5 miles on grass inside track at 6:00 pace. Thursday: Run 10x440 at 70 seconds on track. Friday: 5-8 miles on road. Saturday: Rest. Sunday: Rest.

WINTER TRAINING: Monday: Training is same for all days. Short interval running on a 155 yd. banked track. Repetitions done on the basis of the number of laps. Work-out 5 days a week, only in evenings. Participates in 15-20 individual and 10 relays, outdoors 1 to 3 road races. Indoors, 10 individual and 8 relays. Does not use weight training. Rests 1 to 2 days before competition. Rests 1-2 weeks between track and cross-country seasons. Coached by Fred Foot.

STRATEGY: "Prefer to follow and kick. Will lead, but would not likely do so in big international race."

Silver medalist in 1964 Tokyo Olympic Games 800 meter run. World ranked 1st in 1963, 2nd 1964, 1st 1965, 9th 1966, 8th 1967.


## Ralph Doubell

RALPH DOUGLAS DOUBELL, Melbourne University Athletic Club, Australia. Age 24, 1969.

Bill Crothers

BEST MARKS: Mile, 4:00.5; ¾ mile, 2:56.8 (t); 1000y, 2:05.5 (indoors);
800m., 1:44.3 (world record); 660y, 1:14.7 (t); 400m., 46.4 (t); 300y,
30.4 (t); 220y, 21.9 (t); 100y, 10.0 (t).

PERSONAL STATISTICS: Born February 11, 1945 at Melbourne, Australia.
5'11" tall, 145 lbs. Started racing in 1963 at age 17.

PRE-RACE WARM-UP: 2-3 miles slow jog, 5 minutes calisthenics, 4-5x100y fast
striding. Walk 100y after each.

PRE-TRAINING WARM-UP: 3 miles faster than pre-race warm-up. 5 minutes
calisthenics. Training: Morning workouts, Monday through Thursday—AM
(7:00), 4 miles at easy speed. Evening workouts at 5:30 PM. Monday—
220x440y about 68 seconds (not timed) with 110y jog between. Tuesday—10x880y in 2:16 with 440y jog in 2½ minutes between. Wednesday—50x110y on grass with 30y fast walk between. Total time 32
minutes. Thursday—10x660y in 1:35-1:40 with 440y jog in 2½ minutes
between. Friday—Rest. Saturday—AM (9:30), time trial of either 220y,
300y, 440y, 660y, or 1320y. Then 30x220y with 110y walk between.
Sunday—AM (10:00), time trial of either 220y, 300y, 440y, 660y, or
1320y. Then 20x300y with 140y walk between.

This training is done the year round. PM workouts are usually run in flat soled
shoes on a cinder track without stop watch timing. The Sunday time trial is
usually omitted if a race is run on Saturday. A substitute workout of 10 miles in
55-60 minutes is done when it rains. He takes no warm-down following workouts. During winter he does light weight-training twice weekly. He annually races
25 times outdoors and 5 times indoors.

Doubell is 1968 Olympic 800m champion, and is coached by Franz Stampfl.


## Rudolf Harbig

RUDOLF HARBIG, Dresden Sport Club, Germany.

BEST MARKS: 1500m, 4:01; 1000m, 2:21.5 (world record); 800m, 1:46.6
(world record); 400m, 46.0 (world record); 200m, 21.5; 100m, 10.6.

PERSONAL STATISTICS: Born November 8, 1913 at Dresden, Germany.
Started racing in 1932 at age 19. Terminated racing career in 1942 at age
29. Reported missing in action on Russian front, March 5, 1944.

PRE-TRAINING WARM-UP: Easy jogging for 1¼ miles. In the later years of his
career, this warm-up frequently involved 30-45 minutes easy jogging during winter months.

WINTER TRAINING: Harbig's winter training started in the middle of November, and involved three workouts each week. On Sunday mornings he ran in the forest. Tuesday evenings he trained in the gymnasium, lifting light dumbbells (30-40 lbs), skipping rope, climbing rope, calisthenics, and working on gym apparatus. On Friday nights he ran on the floodlit track of his club. The Sunday morning forest runs during winter involved 90 minutes to 2½-3 hours of running, alternately changing speeds from fast to slow and easy running to hard running. This occasionally involved an hour walking in snow. The following Friday workouts by Harbig have been recorded: 11/19/37: 1¼ mile warm-up. Calisthenics. 1¼ mile at faster speed. 11/26/37: 1200m warm-up. Calisthenics. 1500m run. 100m sprint. 12/3/37: 1¼ mile warm-up. Calisthenics. 1500m run. Jog 15 minutes. 1000m light running with 6x80m fast striding enroute. Calisthenics. 1/28/38: 1 mile warm-up. 3x1200m at ¾ speed. Jog 15 minutes between. Calisthenics. 2x40m sprints. 2/18/38: 2½ miles warm-up. 12x100m acceleration sprints. 500m fast. 12/16/38: 45 minutes jogging. 1000m in 3:05. Jog 15 minutes. 1000m in 3:02. Jog 10 minutes. 1000m in 3:11. 3/30/39: Jog 30 minutes warm-up. 1000m in 2:41. Jog 15 minutes. 600m in 1:32. Jog 10 minutes. 600m in 1:33.

SUMMER TRAINING: 4/13/39: 30 minutes jogging, 3x200m in 23.8, 23.8, 24.3. Walk 5 minutes after. Jog 10 minutes. 600m in 1:25.3. 4/23/39: Jog 30 minutes. 800m in 2:11. Jog 15 minutes. 800m in 2:02. Jog 10 minutes. 600m in 1:28. 5/2/39: Jog 20 minutes. 5x200m in 23.2, 23.8, 24.6, 24.7, 24.2. Walk 5 minutes after each. 6/1/39: Jog 20 minutes. Crouch starts. 2x30m, 2x50m, 2x80m, 1x150m, 1x200m, 1x400m. 7/6/39: Jog 25 minutes. 2x300m in 38.2. Jog 5 minutes between. Jog 10 minutes. 500m in 71. Jog 15 minutes. 200m in 24.0. 7/13/39: Last workout before world record 800m in Milan, Italy, on 7/15/39 (1:46.6): Jog 20 minutes. 600m in 1:27. Jog 10 minutes. 300m in 36.9. Jog 10 minutes. 500m in 66.7. 8/8/39: Last workout before world record 400m in Frankfurt, Germany, on 8/12/39 (46.0): Jog 20 minutes. 3x250m in 30.6, 30.2, 29.8. Jog 10 minutes after each.

Harbig was coached by Woldemer Gerschler. His strength was in his iron willpower. His personal life had no shadows, and he kept no secrets from his coach. Harbig did not drink tea or coffee. He ate oatmeal in the morning, and sandwiches and lots of fruit during the day. He ate nothing three hours prior to a workout and five hours before a race. His usual pre-race meal was usually steak and vegetables with little or no liquid. He used no massage (rub-down) normally, although when racing twice in the same day he had light massage between races. Strong seasoning, alcohol in any form, and tobacco were totally unknown to Harbig. His 400m world record stood from 1939 to 1948, and his 800m record remained on the books from 1939 to 1955.

(Parts of the above training of Harbig were reprinted from Ihr Weg Zum Erfolg, by permission of its author, Toni Nett.)

Rudolf Harbig

# Tomas Jungwirth

TOMAS JUNGWIRTH, Club Sk Slavia, Prague, Czechoslovakia. Age 30 years, 1972.

BEST MARKS: One-hour run, 16.5km (10¼ miles); 2000m., 5:30; 1500m., 3:43.8; 1200m., 2:57.2; 1000m., 2:19.3; 800m., 1:46.7; 600m., 1:16.9; 400m., 47.0; 300m., 34.0; 200m., 22.2; 100m., 11.3.

PERSONAL STATISTICS: Born November 24, 1942 at Prague, Czechoslovakia. 6'1½", 157 lbs. Started racing in 1959 at age 17.

PRE-RACE WARM-UP: 2 or 3km, 20 minutes of calisthenics. and 5x100m. in 14-15 seconds each.

PRE-TRAINING WARM-UP: Same as pre-race warm-up.

TRAINING: No fall training is done.

WINTER TRAINING: Monday—PM, 15km hard fartlek in 1 hour, 3 minutes. Tuesday—AM, 7km easily in 35 minutes. PM, 2km. 800m., in 2:50. Rest 5 minutes. 800m. in 2:24. Rest 5 minutes. 1000m. in 2:55. Rest 5 minutes. 1200m. in 4:27. Rest 5 minutes. 800m. in 2:20. Rest 5 minutes. 600m. in 1:37. 1km easily. Wednesday—PM, 4km jog. 5x200m. in 33 seconds each. Jog 200m. after each. 5x200m. in 40 seconds each. Jog 200m. after each. 5x300m. in 49 seconds each. Jog 200m. after each. Jog 1km. Thursday—AM, 2km. 5x100m. 100m.-100m.-200m. in 32 seconds. Rest 5 minutes. 200m.-200m.-300m. in 49 seconds. Rest 7 minutes. 300m. in 50 seconds. Jog 200m. 300m. in 49 seconds. Jog 200m. 400m. in 64 seconds. Jog 200m. 300m. in 50 seconds. Jog 200m. 300m. in 49 seconds. Jog 200m., 400m. in 59.2 seconds. Friday—PM, 10km jog. Saturday—AM, 2km, Rest 5 minutes. 5x100m. in 16 seconds each. 3 sets of 200m.-200m.-300m. with 200m. jog between runs and ten minutes rest between sets. Times of sets: 35-36-36, 34-34-44, 34-34-42.6 seconds. Sunday—rest.

SPRING/SUMMER TRACK RACING SEASON: Monday—PM, 100m.-100m.-150m. in 20 seconds. Jog 100m. between each. Rest 5 minutes. 100m.-100m.-200m. in 29 seconds. Jog 100m. after each. Rest 5 minutes. 4x250m. in 36-37-35-34.8 seconds. Jog 150m. after each. Rest 10 minutes. 100m.-100m.-150m. in 18 seconds. Jog 100m. after each. 1km easily. Tuesday—AM, 6km cross-country. PM, 9km. 100m. in 13.2 seconds. Rest 3 minutes. 500m. in 1:05.4. Rest 15 minutes. 300m. in 35 seconds. 1km. Wednesday—PM, 9km fartlek. Thursday—PM, 3km. 400m., 400m. In 52.9 seconds. Rest 12 minutes. 400m. in 50.9 seconds. 1km easily. Friday: Rest. Saturday—PM, 3km. Easy 800m. in 1:57.7. 3km slow. Sunday: Competition. (Typical Sunday) 800m. (first) 1:52.8. Rest 40 minutes. 400m. (first) 47.3.

Many-time CCSR champion in 400m. and 800m. Fifth in European championships in 800m. (1:46.7) in 1966. Rests 1½ months after competitive season
before continuing training.

## Larry Kelly

LAWRENCE BYRON KELLY, University of Tennessee. Age 20, 1969.

BEST MARKS: mile, 4:09; 1320y, 3:04; 1000y, 2:10.1; 880y, 1:47.1; 600y,
1:10.1; 440y, 45.5 (r); 220y, 21.8.

PERSONAL STATISTICS: Born May 18, 1947 at Chicago, Illinois. 6'0", 160
lbs. Started racing in 1962 at age 14.

PRE-RACE WARM-UP: About 2 miles of jogging, much stretching, and 20
minutes of short fast runs.

PRE-TRAINING WARM-UP: ½ mile jog.

FALL CROSS-COUNTRY TRAINING: Morning workouts Monday through
Thursday consist of 5-8 mile runs. Warm-up and warm-down for PM workouts are 3 miles each. Monday—20x440y in 65-68 seconds with 1 minute
interval. Tuesday—3xmile in 5:00 and 5x880y in 2:30 with half-distance
jog interval. Wednesday—2 miles in 10:00 and 8x440y in 72 seconds with
440y jog. Thursday—40x220y in 32-35 seconds. Friday—warm-up only.
Saturday—Race. Sunday—10-15 mile run.

WINTER TRAINING: Monday—1320y in 3:10-3:15 and 20x220y in 28-29
seconds. Tuesday—660y in 1:20-1:22 and 8x330y in 38-41 seconds.
20x110y untimed. Wednesday—10x440y in 63-65 seconds and 20x150y
with 70y jog between 150's. Thursday: 2x(8x220y in 26-27 seconds) and
4x100y shuttle run. Friday—light workout. Saturday—Race. Sunday—5-10
mile run.

SPRING/SUMMER TRAINING: Monday—15x330y in 39-41 seconds and
20x110 in 14-15 seconds. Tuesday—660y in 1:20 and 2x(8x220y in 26-27
seconds). Wednesday—1320y in 3:05-3:10 and 20x220y in 28-29 seconds.
3 mile jog. Thursday—10x220y in 27-28 seconds. Friday—warm-up only.
Saturday—Race. Sunday—Rest.

Kelly in 1964 and '65 set four national prep records: 600y, 1:13.1; 880y,
1:50.4; 2 mile relay, 7:47.0; and 880y indoors, 1:52.0. In 1967 he ran third in
both the NCAA and AAU 880y. He preferred to lead with a quick pace. He
usually ran 12 indoor, 11 outdoor, and 8 cross-country races annually. He ran

two workouts per day only in the fall and rested two weeks following that training period.

Larry Kelly

George Kerr

## George Kerr

GEORGE KERR, University of Illinois, Jamaica, and West Indies Federation. Age 22, 1959.

BEST MARKS: Mile, 4:24; ¾ mile, 3:10.0; 880y, 1:47.8; 800m., 1:46.4; 660y, 1:18.2; 600y, 1:10.6; 440y, 46.1; 400m, 46.1; 330y, 33.8; 220y, 21.3; 200m, 21.6; 100m, 10.5; 100y, 9.9 seconds.

PERSONAL STATISTICS: Born October 16, 1937 in Jamaica. 5'11", 154 lbs. Started racing in 1955 at age 17.

PRE-RACE WARM-UP: Begin 40-45 minutes before race. Jog ¾ mile. Walk 440 yds. Stride 440 yds. easily. Calisthenics. 2-3x50-60 yds. sprints.

PRE-TRAINING WARM-UP: Jog one mile. Walk 440y. Stride 440y easily. Calisthenics, 1-2x50-60y sprints.

WINTER TRAINING (December, 1959): Workouts during this period are timed over accurately marked grass area. Monday—2x¾m in 3:20. Walk and jog 15 minutes between. Tuesday—12x220y in 30 seconds. Jog 220y in 2½ minutes after each. Wednesday—3x660y in 1:30. Jog 5 minutes after each. Thursday—5x330y in 42 seconds. Jog 4 minutes after each. Friday—4x440y in 60 seconds. Jog and walk 5 minutes after each. Saturday—2x880y in 2:10. Jog and walk 7-8 minutes between. Sunday—Rest.

SPRING TRAINING (April, 1960). Workouts during this period timed on cinder track. Monday—¾ mile in 3:10-15. Walk and jog 15 minutes. 4x110 in 12.5. Walk 110y after each. Tuesday—6x220y in 27 seconds each. Jog 220y in 2½ minutes after each. Wednesday—660y in 1:19. Walk and jog 15 minutes. 330y in 35 seconds. Thursday—4x220y in 25 seconds. Walk and jog 220y in 3 minutes after each. Friday—Jog 10 minutes. Calisthenics. 2x110y in 12.5. Saturday—Race. Sunday—Rest.

Kerr jogs ¾ mile as a warm-down after each workout. Most of his workouts are timed, either by a coach, or by himself carrying a stopwatch as he runs. Duration of workouts—45-60 minutes, starting at 4:00 PM daily. Normally his competitive season begins in February and ends in July or August. He rests from competition during August, September, and October, and starts his Winter training program in November. During vacation periods when he has no classes at the University of Illinois, Kerr runs two miles in approximately 10 minutes each morning in addition to his usual daily training. He seldom depends upon pre-arranged tactics in his races, usually "goes with the pace," prefers an evenly paced 880y race, and has a terrific finishing "wallop." He eats 3½ to 4 hours prior to racing. Kerr uses no weight training as such.

*George Kerr ran 1:46.1 for the 1960 bronze medal at Rome. Four years later his 1:45.9 was good for fourth place at Tokyo.*

# John Lilly

JOHN ERNEST LILLY, Oregon State University and Athens Athletic Club of Oakland, California. Age 20 years, 1968.

BEST MARKS: 2-miles, 9:22.0 (t); 1-mile, 4:07.0 (t); 1500m, 3:58.1; ¾-mile, 3:02.2 (t); 1000y, 2:09.9 (indoors); 2:07.8 (outdoors); 800m, 1:48.7; 880y, 1:48.4; 660y, 1:18.8 (t); 440y, 48.6 and 47.6 (r); 330y, 35.8 (t); 220y, 22.8, 100y, 10.2.

PERSONAL STATISTICS: Born November 2, 1968 at Stockton, California. 5'9", 140 lbs. Started racing in 1962 at age 14.

PRE-RACE WARM-UP: Jog about ½ mile, stop and stretch vigorously for 5-8 minutes, either jog or run not more than 5 slow 80-100y sprints in flats. Switch to spikes for some quick speed bursts.

PRE-TRAIN WARM-UP: Jog one mile, stretching exercises for 10-20 minutes, with spikes run 5 or less build-up 110's.

FALL CROSS-COUNTRY TRAINING: Trains 1 workout per day, four days per week with Friday, Saturday, and Sunday, reserved for travel, competition, and rest respectively. Monday—1x1320 faster than race pace, 6x660 in 1:40-1:45 with 2-3 minute intervals. Tuesday—10 miles on road in 58 minutes followed by weight training session of bench presses, sit-ups, and curls. Wednesday—6x440 in 68-70 seconds with 110y interval jog, 4x220 in 28-32 seconds with 50y interval jog, 4x440 in 68-70 seconds with 110y interval jog. Thursday—20-30 minutes jog and weight training.

WINTER TRAINING: All running outside despite weather, training hard early in the week with Thursday through Saturday reserved for travel and competition and Sunday for rest. Monday—AM, warm-up, short pick-ups, 20x220y with two 110y jog intervals run slow-fast. PM, 1x660 all-out at about 1:20.0, 1x165y hard, 1 mile jog. Tuesday—AM, only 4x330y, 4x220, 4x165 all hard, 1 mile jog. Wednesday—1x550 all-out at about 64 seconds, 10x110y of easy striding, jog 1 mile.

SPRING/SUMMER TRAINING: Trains hard early in week on track, eases training with fartlek sessions later in week, competes on Saturday, and totally rests on Sunday. Monday—AM, 1 mile jog, 3-4 short accelerated sprints. PM, 4x440y in 57-59 seconds running relaxed with 2-3 minute interval, 10 minutes of rest-jog, 5x330 acceleration sprints starting easy and finishing fast, 5x110 acceleration sprints. Tuesday—20-25 minutes of hard fartlek on grass and trails, 1x110y sprints on grass. Wednesday—AM, 1 mile jog, 3-4 accelerated springs. PM, 4x220 at 25-26 seconds with 50y walk intervals, 440 walk repeat 4x220y 25-26 second intervals. Thursday—20-25 minutes fartlek. Friday—2 miles easy fartlek. Saturday—Compete. Sunday—Rest.

Coached by Berny Wagner at Oregon State and Jim Luttrell at San Carlos High School, California, John was the national jr. champ at 880y in 1966 at age 18 and the 1969 Pacific—8 Conference runner-up. John is an advocate of weight training in the non-track season working out twice weekly with bench presses 3x10 at 110-120-130 lbs. and curls 3x10 at 40-50-60 lbs.

During the track season John favors hard training early in the week, with at least a day's rest before dual meets and 2 or 3 days rest before major competition. In his specialty, the 880y run, he prefers to run from the back of the pack, surging on the last back stretch, and sprinting the last 100 yards.

*John Lilly's best 800m. came in 1970 with a 1:47.7.*

John Lilly

# Juris Luzins

JURIS LUZINS, William and Mary University, Virginia. Age 22, 1969.

BEST MARKS: 2 miles, 9:29.0; mile, 4:05.7 (indoors); ¾ mile, 2:56.2; 1000y, 2:05.6 (indoors); 880y, 1:46.4; 660y, 1:19.0 (t); 440y, 47.9 (r); 220y, 23.5 (t); 100y, 10.7 (t).

PERSONAL STATISTICS: Born June 22, 1947 in Germany. 6'2", 167 lbs. Started racing in 1963 at age 15.

PRE-RACE WARM-UP: 1-mile jog. Calisthenics. Then 6-8x110y accelerations, running the last two very fast.

PRE-TRAINING WARM-UP: Jog 1½ mile. Calisthenics. 4x110y acceleration run. 4x110y acceleration sprints. Walk briefly after each.

FALL CROSS-COUNTRY TRAINING: Morning workouts: Monday through Thursday—AM (8:00), 3-5 miles in 7 minutes per mile. Evening training (3:00). Monday—15 miles at 6:30 per mile. Then 10x110y in 15 seconds. Jog 110y between. Tuesday—8x880y in 2:20-2:25. Jog 889y between. Or, 3x1-mile in 4:40-4:45. Jog 880y between. Wednesday—6-8 miles alternating 1 minute at race pace and 1 minute jogging. Thursday—10x110y, 10x220y, 10x110y, 10x220y run at 29-30 seconds per 220 pace on grass. Jog an equal distance after each. Friday—Warm-up, stretching, walking and easy striding. Total 4-5 miles. Saturday—5-mile race. Sunday—AM, 8-10 miles in 7 minutes per mile pace. PM, Rest.

WINTER TRAINING: (On 160y per lap wooden track outdoors.) Monday—4-miles at 5:30-6:00 per mile. 10x110y in 15 seconds. Jog 110y after each. Tuesday—12x80y at ¾ full speed, 2x660y in 1:21 and 1:25. Jog 880y between. 10x160y in 19-20 seconds. Walk-jog 160y between. Or 1320y in 3:02-3:05 instead of the 660's. Wednesday—12x80y acceleration runs. 5x440y in 53-55 seconds. Walk-jog 4 minutes between. Thursday—12x80y acceleration sprints. Then 9-12x220y in 26-27 seconds. Walk-jog 2 minutes between. Friday—Calisthenics. Alternate walking and easy striding. Total 4-5 miles. Saturday—Race. Sunday—4-5 miles easy running.

SPRING/SUMMER TRAINING: Monday—4-5 miles in 5:30-6:00 minutes per mile. 10x110y in 14-15 seconds. Jog 110y between. 1320y in 3:00. Walk 10 minutes. Then 440y in 53 seconds. Walk 10 minutes. 8x220y in 27-28 seconds. Jog 220y after each. Tuesday—8x110y in 12-13 seconds. Walk 5 minutes. Then 5x440y in 53-54 seconds. Walk-jog 5 minutes between. Or, 1x550y in 1:05. Jog 440y. 1x330y in 38 seconds. Jog 440y. 5x160y in 18-19 seconds. Walk jog 160y between. Wednesday—8x110y in 12-13 seconds. Walk 110y between. 3x330y in 36-38 seconds. Walk-jog 5 minutes between. 2x220y in 25-26 seconds. Walk-jog 220y between. Thursday—8x110y in 12-13 seconds. Walk 110y between. 8-12x220y in

25-26 seconds. Walk-jog 3 minutes between. Or, 10x110y, 10x220y and 10x110y at speed of 28.5 per 220y on grass. Jog an equal distance after each. Friday—Warm-up. Calisthenics. Alternate walking and easy striding. Total 4-5 miles. Saturday—Race. Sunday—Rest.

Each evening workout is concluded by jogging 2 miles as a warm-down. He does weight training regularly, and he competes in 10 indoor, 10 outdoor, and 10 cross-country races per year. He has been coached by Leo Schutte, Harry Groves, John Randolph, and Ashton Lodley.

*Luzins ranked 5th in the world in 1969 and improved to 1:45.2 in 1971 when he was rated as America's best two-lapper. His 2:05.6 1000 in 1970 set an American indoor record. In 1972 he had a 3:58.2 mile.*

Josef Plachy, Ralph Doubell, Juris Luzins

# Manfred Matuschewski

MANFRED MATUSCHEWSKI, East Germany. Age 23, 1962.

BEST MARKS: 1500m, 3:40.2; 800m, 1:45.7; 400m, 47.9; 200m, 22.4; 100m, 10.8.

PERSONAL STATISTICS: Born 1939, started racing in 1956 at age 17. His months of training, which include more than just running, are divided into sections. After each section are listed the number of days that that particular activity is participated in during the month.

JANUARY TRAINING 1960: (1) Rest: 3 days. (2) Skiing: 7 days, about 110 total miles. (3) Indoor training: 8 days, 2 hours each consisting of calisthenics and strength training. (4) Running: 13 days. The running training is divided into 3 basic areas; (1) Speedwork: 3 days, 3½ total miles. (2) Specialized endurance: 8 days, 28½ total miles. (3) General endurance: 2 days, 10 miles total, also 8 times swimming is added to the running. Following are examples of the 3 types of running training during this month. I Speedwork: 2x(9x110) with flying start in 13-13.5 seconds, 1-1½ minute walk after each. II Speedwork: 6x33y flying start, 6x55y, 8x110 flying start in 13-13.5. I Specialized endurance: 20x220 flying start in 31-33 seconds, 1 minute walk after each. II Specialized endurance: 3x(6x220) in 29-32 seconds, 1½ minute walk after each. General endurance: 1½ hours of fartlek at distances from 440-1100.

MARCH TRAINING 1960: (1) Rest: 8 days. (2) Indoor training: Same as January, 2 days. (3) Running: 18 days; (A) Speedwork: 4 days, 4½ miles total. (B) Specialized endurance: 8 days, 21 total miles. (C) General endurance: 6 days, 28 total miles, also 8 times swimming. Examples of workouts during March: I Speed work: 110's with flying start in 12.5-13 seconds, rest 1 minute after each. II Speedwork: 2x(5x220) flying start in 26.8-27.1 seconds, walk 2 minutes after each. III Speedwork: 6x33y, 6x55y, 8x150 near 100%. I Specialized endurance: 20x220 in 28-30 seconds, 1 minute rest after each. II Specialized endurance: 2x(20x110y in 14-15 seconds.) Walk 20 seconds after each. III Specialized endurance: 5x440 flying start in 61-62 seconds, 4 minute walk after each, 5x330y in 45-46 seconds. Walk 2½ minutes after each. 5x220 flying start in 28-30 seconds, rest 1½ minutes after each and 5 minutes between set. General endurance: Same as January.

MAY TRAINING 1960: (1) Rest: 4 days. (2) Traveling: 2 days. (3) Track meets: 7 days. (4) Games: 2 days, 1½ hours each. (5) Walking: 1 day for 1½ hours. (6) Running: 15 days; (A) Speedwork: 8 days, 6 miles total. (B) Specialized endurance: 4 days, 6¼ miles total. (C) General endurance: 3 days, 14 miles total.

Examples of workouts during May—I Speedwork: 2x(6x110) flying start in 12-12.5 seconds, walk 45-60 seconds after each. II Speedwork: 2x(5x110) in 11.2-11.9 seconds, 1 minute rest after each, 3 minute interval between sets,

5x220 in 25-26 seconds with 2½ minute rest after each. III Speedwork: 10 starts, 5x55y, 3x110 in 11.3 seconds, 2 minute rest after each, 2x220 in 25-25.5 seconds, rest 2½ after each. I Specialized endurance: 8x110 in 12-13 seconds, 1 minute after each, 2x(4x220) in 25-28 seconds, 1½ minute rest after each and 4 minute between sets. II Specialized endurance: 5x440 in 58, 55, 54, 54, 53 seconds, rest 3-4 minutes after each. III Specialized endurance: 3x(5x220) in 26.5-28 seconds, 1½ minute after each and 3-4 minutes between sets. General endurance: Same as January.

The following was Matuschewski's training 10 days prior to the 1960 Olympic 800m. August 22—AM, 6x330 flying start in 42-1.42.5 seconds, rest 2 minutes after each. PM, 4x110 flying start in 10.4-10.6 seconds, walk 110 after each. August 23—AM, 2 hours of relaxed walking. PM, Canoeing on river. August 24—AM, 6x110 in 12.5 seconds, rest 20 seconds after each, 6x220 flying start in 27-5-28 seconds, 30 seconds after each. PM, 4x110 in 10.5-11.5 seconds, 30-40 seconds after each. August 25—AM. Rest PM, 3x440 in 49.4-50.0 seconds, 7-8 minute walk after each. August 26—AM, 40 minute easy fartlek. PM, Canoeing on river. August 27—AM, 30 minute calisthenics. PM, 10x110 flying start in 10.10.9 seconds, walk 110 after each. August 28: Travel to Rome. August 29—AM, 2 mile jog. PM, 6x220 in 28 seconds, 1 minute rest after each. August 30—AM, 2 mile jog. PM, 10x110 in 13 seconds, 1 minute rest after each. August 31—Olympic 800m. round, 3rd place, 1:51.0; second round, 3rd place, 1:48.1. September 1, semi-final, 3rd place, 1:47.4. September 2, final, 6th place, 1:52.0.

*"Matu" was the European 800m. Champion in 1962 and 1966, and the European Cup 800m. and 1500m., titlist in 1967. A brilliant world class runner for many years, he recorded his best times near the end of his career. He ranked second internationally in 1963, 3rd in 1966 and 1969, 5th in 1967.*

Left, Manfred Matuschewski

## Roger Moens

ROGER MOENS, Brussels, Belgium. Age 28, 1958.

BEST MARKS: Mile, 3:58.9; 1500m, 3:44.0; 1000m, 2:19.6; 800m, 1:45.7
  (world record); 400m, 47.3; 880, 1:48.3.

PERSONAL STATISTICS: Born April 26, 1930. 5'10¾", 156 lbs. Started racing
  in 1947 at age 17.

PRE-RACE WARM-UP: Jog 30 minutes. 5x110m fast striding. Walk briefly after
  each. 250-300m sprint.

PRE-TRAINING WARM-UP: Jog 30 minutes. 5x100 fast. Walks. In January,
  1959, Moens described his training as follows:

WINTER TRAINING: Monday & Friday: 10x440 in 57. Jog 400m in 1½
  minutes after each. Tuesday & Saturday: 10x220m in 24.5 avg. Jog 400m
  in 3 minutes after. Wednesday: 10x300m in 39. Jog 400m in 3 minutes
  after. Thursday: 3x600m in 1:24. Jog 800m in 6 minutes after each.
  Sunday: Rest.

SUMMER TRAINING: (With a race on Sunday, train 4 days during the week.
  Rest either one or two days prior to each race.) Day (1): 6x200m in 23.
  Jog 4 minutes after each. Day (2): 8x300m in 38. Jog 4 minutes after
  each. Day (3): 6x400m in 54. Jog 5 minutes after each. Day (4): 10x100m
  in approximately 11.4. Jog 2 minutes after each. (Each workout is followed by a 10 minute warm-down.)

The following description of his training was given to Australian Allan Lawrence
by Moens in 1957:

WINTER TRAINING: Seven days per week, repeat the following workouts in
  succession: Day (1): 30x200m in 29. Jog 150m after each. Day (2):
  10x440m in 58. Jog 400m after each. Day (3): 15x300m in 44. Jog 300m
  after each.

SPRING TRAINING: (7 days per week, repeat following workouts in succession.): Day (1): 30x100m in 13. Jog 300m after each. (Use running start
  for each 100m.) Day (2): 10x400m in 57. Jog 400m after each. Day (3):
  10x300m in 42. Jog 300m after each.

SUMMER TRAINING (before starting intense racing season): Day (1):
  20x100m in 12. Jog 300m after each. Day (2): 6x440m in 53. Jog 400m
  after each. Day (3): 8x300m in 39. Jog 4 minutes after each. (Repeat
  these workouts in successive order.)

Duration of workouts: 1½-2 hours, starting at 5:00 PM. Moens never trains more than once daily. Does not use weight lifting. He participates in 3 cross-country and approximately 25 track races annually. Moens established his world 800m record at Oslo, Norway, August 3, 1955. He is a Police Judicare of the Brussels Police Department. Moens participated in an intense summer racing season of three months in which he raced as often as 5 times per week.

*Moens was silver medalist in the 1960 Olympic 800m.*

Roger Moens

# Robert Ouko

ROBERT STEPHEN OUKO, Kenya and North Carolina Central University, Durham, North Carolina. Age 23 years, 1971.

BEST MARKS: 1500m., 3:49.3 (t); ¾ mile, 2:54.3 (t); 1000m., 2:16; 800m, 1:46.6; 600m, 1:16; 400m, 45.8; 440 yards, 46.9; 300m., 33.4; 200m, 21.3; 100m., 10.8; 100 yards, 10.0.

PERSONAL STATISTICS: Born October 24, 1948 at Kisii, Kenya. 5'9". Started racing in 1967 at age 19.

PRE-RACE WARM-UP: Jog 10 minutes, 10-15 minutes of exercises, jog 20 minutes, 3-4x150y., rest 10 minutes.

PRE-TRAINING WARM-UP: Jog 20 minutes, 5 minutes speedwork, striding, exercises. 2-mile warm-down following workouts.

SPRING/SUMMER TRACK RACING SEASON: Monday—AM (6:30), 60 minutes fartlek. PM 8x150m. at half speed. Tuesday—100m. progressions from 100m. up to 800m. and back down, all at ¾ speed. Wednesday—AM, 4-mile run in 30 minutes. PM, 4x400m. in 68 seconds, jog 5 minutes, 6x300m. at ¾ speed. Thursday—AM, 60 minutes fartlek. PM, 20x200m. in 32 seconds. Friday—Rest. Saturday—Race or time trial. Sunday—Easy jogging on grass.

Does no weight training. Coached by Bob Hancock and Dr. L.T. Walker. 1970 British Commonwealth 800m. champion. Anchorman on Kenyan world record holding 2-mile relay team. He ranked 10th in 1970, 7th in 1971. *He recorded a lifetime best of 1:46.0 in 1972 and placed fifth in the '72 Olympic final.*


# Josef Plachy

JOSEF PLACHY, Club East Slovakia Iron Works, Kosice, Czechoslovakia. Age 23 years, 1972.

BEST MARKS: 1500m., 3:57.6; 1000m., 2:18.5; 1000y (indoors), 2:06.7; 880y, 1:46.7; 800m. 1:45.4; 400m. 47.3; 300m., 35.6t.

PERSONAL STATISTICS: Born February 28, 1949 at Kosice, Czechoslovakia. 5'11½", 161 lbs. Started racing in 1965 at age 16. Plans to continue racing until 1978 at age 28.

PRE-RACE WARM-UP: 15 minutes continuous running (3km), 15 minutes gymnastics, 3x110m. sprints. After introduction to crowd 4x60m. on racing track.

PRE-TRAINING WARM-UP: Before every training session, 5km in 20 minutes followed by ten minutes of gymnastics.

FALL CROSS-COUNTRY TRAINING: Monday—PM (3:00), 10x600m. in 1:37 each. Walk 2 minutes after each. 20 minutes continuous running. Tuesday—PM (3:00), 5x300m. in 45 seconds each. Jog 100m. after each. 4 minutes rest. 5x300m. in 47 seconds each. Jog 100m. after each. Rest 4 minutes. 5x300m. in 45 seconds each. Jog 100m. after each. 20 minutes continuous running. Wednesday—PM (3:00), 12km fartlek in the forest. On track 20x100m. with short intervals. 15 minutes continuous running. Thursday—PM (3:00), 4 sets of 200m.-200m.-400m.-600m. in 30-30-56-1:40 each. Jog 100m. after each. 15 minutes continuous run. Friday—PM (3:00), 16km fartlek. Saturday—AM (10:00), 8km fartlek. PM (3:00), 2 sets of 6x200m. in 28 seconds each. 20 minutes endurance running. Sunday—AM (10:00), 10km fartlek. PM (3:00), 2 sets of 3x600m. in 1:38 each. 15 minutes endurance running.

WINTER TRAINING: In the winter he does not race and so trains six days a week. Monday—PM (3:00), 18km fartlek. Tuesday—PM (2:00), 20km ski-running. Wednesday—AM (10:00), 10km fartlek. PM (2:00), gymnastics in the gymnasium. Thursday—PM (2:00), 5km run with teammates. 4x3000m. in 9:15 each. Jog 400m. after each. Friday—PM (2:00), 22km fartlek. Saturday—Rest. Sunday—Ski-running with teammates.

SPRING/SUMMER TRACK RACING SEASON: Monday—AM (10:00), 8km run. PM (3:00), 4 sets of 4x150m. in 22 seconds each. Tuesday—AM (10:00), 8km run. PM (3:00), 3 sets of 150m.-150m.-200m.-300m. in 21-21-28-43 seconds each. Wednesday—AM (10:00), 8km run. PM (3:00), 2x400m. in 48 seconds each. Gun starts in curve, 120m. sprints. Thursday—PM (3:00), 3x1500m. with 4 minutes rest after each (run for endurance.) Friday—12km fartlek in forest. Saturday—Rest. Sunday—Competition.

In winter, work is done with rings and bars in gymnasium as well as some weight lifting. He set the European record for 880 yards in 1970, and won the Americas/Europe 800 meters in 1:45.4. He was ranked first in the world that year. Plachy has Olympic experience having run in the Mexico City games, finishing 5th in the final. He races 25 times a year and trains year round with no rest after his racing season.

## Kevin Reabe

KEVIN CLYDE REABE, Kettering High School, Michigan. Age 17 years, 1969.

BEST MARKS: 2-mile, 10.00; 1-mile, 4:19; 880, 1:52.4; 440, 48.6; 220, 21.9; 100, 10.3.

PERSONAL STATISTICS: Born June 25, 1952 in Pontiac, Michigan. 6'2'', 152 lbs. Started racing in 1967 at age 14.

PRE-RACE WARM-UP: Start 45 minutes before race. Run 1 mile. Rest 10 minutes. Alternate running 440's and stretching for 15 minutes. Jog to start.

PRE-TRAINING WARM-UP: Jog 2 miles. Stretch for 5 minutes. Cross-Country: Run 6 miles every morning. Monday, Tuesday, Wednesday, Friday, and Saturday: 10x440 in 64. Rest 90. Hill sprints. Thursday: 8-10x880 in 2.30. Rest 90. Hill sprints. Sunday: 6 mile run in 36 minutes.

WINTER: Everyday run 5 miles in 30 minutes. 10x50 strides.

SPRING: Everyday run 6 miles in the morning. Monday: 10-15x300 in 40. Jog 140. Hill work. Tuesday: Same. Wednesday, Thursday, Saturday, and Sunday: 10-15x220 in 27. Walk for 1 minute. 5-10 by 100 hard. Friday: 10x440 in 58-60. 2-3 minute walk.

Trains at 5:30 AM (45 minutes) and 2 PM (1½ hours). Coached by Charles Griffith and Howard Heitzeg. In 1969 Kevin won the Michigan State meet, Junior Olympic, and National Junior Champs 880's. Participates in 19 cross-country, 4 indoor, and 40 outdoor races annually. Rests for 2 months after cross-country season.

*In 1970, Reabe ran 1:50.6 while still a prep. He entered Kansas University that fall and switched to Michigan State in 1972.*

Josef Plachy

Peter Scott

## Ralph Schultz

RALPH CHRISTOPHER SCHULTZ, Northwestern University and University of Chicago Track Club. Age 22 years, 1969.

BEST MARKS: 3-miles, 14:50; 2-miles, 9:28; mile, 4:08; 1000y, 2:06.0; 880y, 1:47.3; 660y, 1:17; 440y, 47.3 (relay); 220y, 22.0 (t).

PERSONAL STATISTICS: Born June 4, 1947 at Chicago, Illinois. 6'1", 177 lbs. Started racing in 1962 at age 14.

PRE-RACE WARM-UP: Easy jogging followed by ¾-mile of faster jogging, light stretching, 4x110y increasing speed, rest, short sprints and more easy jogging.

PRE-TRAINING WARM-UP: ¾-1½-miles at increasing pace, light stretching, a few 100y sprints. Fall cross-country training: Monday: 20x440y in 70-80 seconds with 60-90 seconds rest or 6x880y in 2:20-2:35 with 3-4 minutes rest on golf course. Tuesday: 6-7-mile run, fast pace at end. Wednesday: 3-4x1-mile in 4:50-5:20 with 8-9 minute rest. Thursday: 4-mile fartlek. Friday: 2-mile easy jog. Saturday: 5-mile race. Sunday: Rest or 3-5-mile run in forest.

WINTER TRAINING: Monday: 2x(5x330y in 43-45 seconds with 110y jog interval) with 220y walk between sets, or ¾-mile in 3:05 and 660y in 1:23. Tuesday: 4x5 minutes fast run in flats with 3 minute rest. Wednesday: In early season, 10x440y in 61-62 seconds with 220y jog interval or 4x880y in 2:04 with 660y walk-jog. In late season, 3x440y in 54, 51, 55 seconds with 5 minutes rest. Thursday: 2-3 miles of easy fartlek. Friday: Easy warm-up. Saturday: Race. Sunday: Rest or 1½-mile easy jog.

SPRING TRAINING: Monday: 2x880y in 2:03 and 1:55 with 10 minutes rest, or ¾-mile in 3:06 and 440y in 51 seconds. Tuesday: 3-4x440y in 53-54 seconds with 550y jog-walk interval. Wednesday: 3x330y in 35-37 seconds with 7 minute rest, or 10x220y in 26-27 seconds with 220y jog. Thursday: 3 miles of easy fartlek. Friday: Easy jogging. Saturday: Race. Sunday: Rest or easy jogging.

Schultz's 2:06.0 1000y in 1969 unofficially tied the world indoor record. His best times in high school were 49.5, 1:52.6, and 4:19.9 in the 440 yards, 880 yards, and mile respectively. He prefers the racing strategy of "follow and kick." He has been coached by Bob Ehrhart, John Megson, and Ted Haydon. He is a three-time Big 10 champion.

# Peter Scott

PETER LAWRENCE SCOTT, University of Nebraska and Boston A.A. Age 25 years, 1968.

BEST MARKS: 2-miles, 9:17.6; mile, 4:09.6; ¾-mile, 3:02.2; 1000y, 2:10.5; 880y, 1:47.6; 660y, 1:18.4; 440y, 48.1; 220y, 22.2; 100y, 10.2.

PERSONAL STATISTICS: Born March 3, 1943 in Connecticut. 5'8½", 148 lbs. Started racing in 1960 at age 17. Terminated racing in 1967 at age 25.

PRE-RACE WARM-UP: 1-mile very slow jog, 15 minutes of stretching exercises, 10x80y in 11 seconds with 100y walk after each.

PRE-TRAINING WARM-UP: 1-mile jog, stretching exercises, 5x80y with 80y walk after each.

FALL CROSS-COUNTRY TRAINING: Monday: 8-10-mile run at 6:20 per mile pace or 5-6-mile run at 5:50 pace. Tuesday: 20x440y in 63-66 seconds with 110y jog interval, or 10x880y in 2:15-2:20 with 440y jog interval. Wednesday: 5x1-mile in 4:45-4:50 with 880y jog, or 8x¾-mile in 3:30-3:35 with 880y jog. Thursday: 5x(660y, 440y, 330y, 220y) untimed. Friday: 3-5-mile jog at 7:00 pace. Saturday: Race. Sunday: Rest or 6 miles at 6:30 pace.

WINTER TRAINING: Monday: 10x440 in 59-60 seconds with 250y jog interval. Tuesday: 3x660y in 1:24-1:25, or ¾-mile in 3:08 and 3x330y in 39 seconds. Wednesday: 3x880y in 1:58-2:03 with 10 minute walk between. Thursday: 6-12x220y in 25-30 seconds with 250y jog (if important race upcoming, 4-5x220y fast). Friday: 2-mile jog and 6-8x50y at easy pace. Saturday: Race. Sunday: Rest or 6 miles at 6:30-6:50 pace.

SPRING/SUMMER TRAINING: Monday: 4-5x440y in 53.5-55.0 seconds., or 3x440y in 50 seconds with 10 minute rest between. Tuesday: 3x660y in 1:22-1:23.5, or 1x¾-mile in 3:03-3:05.5, or 1x(660y, 440y, 220y) in 1:20, 50 seconds, and 36 seconds. Wednesday: 10x220y in 24-25.5 seconds with 220y jog-walk between. Thursday: 3-mile jog and 6-10x110y in 12.5 seconds. Friday: Rest. Saturday: Race. Sunday: 6-mile jog at 7:00 per mile.

Scott did limited weight training during the fall. His warm-down consisted of an 880y jog and 6x50y sprints. He rested from training one month following the track racing season. In 1966 he won the NCAA 880y and placed 4th in the AAU. As a prep, he was New England and Massachusetts schoolboy 880 champ, with best times of 1:52.8 and 49.4. He was coached by Bill Smith and Frank Sevigne.

# Christian Wägli

CHRISTIAN WÄGLI, Switzerland. Age 26 years. 1960.

BEST MARKS: 800m., 1:47.5; 400m., 47.3; 1000m., 2:23.4; 400m. hurdles, 53.4.

PERSONAL STATISTICS: Born December 22, 1934 at Muri-Gumligen, Switzerland. 6'½" (1.84m), 154 lbs. (70kg.). Started racing at the age of 19 in 1953.

PRE-RACE WARM-UP: Commence about 1½ hours before the race. Easy warm-up with light gymnastics (exercises) during the run. 10 minutes easy gymnastics on the spot. Runs with increasing speed over 100 and 200m. with 50-70% effort. 10 minutes gymnastics. 2-3 runs over 200m. with 80% effort. Easy warm-down and change of clothes during the run. 10 minutes concentrated gymnastics. Light trotting with runs with steady increase of speed over 80-100m. Then follows the main part of the training.

PRE-COMPETITIVE (WINTER) TRAINING: Monday: On track or grass. Long warm-up (45 minutes) combined with gymnastics either during the run or on the spot. 4 runs with gradually increasing speed over 80-100m. 3x300 or 400m. with 75% effort. 15 minutes warm-down. Tuesday: Indoors. 30 minutes warm-up, combined with plenty of gymnastics and exercises with a partner. Jumping exercises for strengthening the legs. Exercises with the medicine-ball or at the wall bars. Exercises to test reaction (starts, etc.). At the end another 10 minutes ball play. Thursday: Track or grass/indoors. Basic warm-up through gymnastics and running. Work with light weights (about 15 minutes). Outside: 6 runs with steady increase of speed over 80-100m.=3 circuits of 400m. track. 5x200m. each followed by 600m. jogging. 15 minutes warm-down. Saturday: Track or on grass; 30 minutes warm-up combined with gymnastics. 4 runs with steady increase in speed over 80-100m. 5x250m, 10 minutes, jogging, 2x600m., basic warm-down.

COMPETITIVE SEASON (SUMMER) TRAINING: Tuesday: Track—20 minutes. Warm-up combine with gymnastics. 4 runs over 100m. with steady increase of speed. 3x200m. in 25 seconds, 10 minutes, jogging, 2x300m. in 39-40 seconds. 10 minutes jogging. 1x600m. in about 1:25 seconds, 15 minutes jogging. Massage and shower. Thursday: Track—20 minutes warm-up combined with gymnastics. 4x100m. runs with steady increase of speed. 3x200m. in 24-25 seconds. 15 minutes jogging. 1x600 or 800m. trial run in about 1:23 or 1:53 minutes. Basic warm-down, massage and shower. Friday: Track or on grass. 30 minutes warm-up, combined with gymnastics. Easy runs with increasing speed over 150 to 200m. 1x300 or 400m. in about 37 or 50 seconds. 15 minutes warm-down. Massage and shower. Saturday: Race. Sunday: About 90-100 minutes cross-country running with variations of pace combined with gymnastics.

"For the last two years I have unfortunately, through reasons connected with my job, not been able to train 4-6 times per week. At the moment, even though the Olympics are coming soon, I have to content myself with 2 or 3 training periods in the week which by and large are made up as I have shown. I have put my profession in first place always and sport must therefore sometimes suffer which means that my training cannot be regular enough or complete enough."

Christian eats his last meal 4-5 hours before a race. He usually has soup, easily digestible meat, and a little salad. He runs no indoor races, but competes in 18-20 outdoor races per year. He rests one day only before races. His workouts last 75-90 minutes from 18.30 to 20.30 hours (6:30-8:30 PM). He rests for 4 months between seasons and runs no cross country races in the fall. Weight training is done with relatively light weights with stress on quick movements. He notes that young runners often lack suppleness but they don't like gymnastics. Because of this, exercises with a partner are highly recommended, for the partner is obliged to take part. Through training on his own so often he is used to having no one in front of him when running. This has dictated his strategy, as is in most cases he sets the pace, by choice. Christian placed 5th in the 800m. run in the Rome Olympics in 1960.

Ralph Schultz

Christian Wägli

## Mark Winzenried

MARK STEVEN WINZENRIED, University of Wisconsin. Age 19 years, 1968.

BEST MARKS: 1500m, 3:46.6; ¾-mile, 2:58.3; 880y, 1:46.5 (r); 800m., 1:46.5; 660y, 1:16.6; 600m., 1:14.8; 440y, 46.3; 220y, 21.8; 100y, 10.1.

PERSONAL STATISTICS: Born October 13, 1949 at Monroe, Wisconsin. 6'2", 165 lbs. Started racing in 1964 at age 14.

PRE-RACE WARM-UP: 1-mile jog, 5-minutes stretching exercises. 6-8x100y pickups, more jogging and stretching if still tight.

PRE-TRAINING WARM-UP: This varies from as little as ¼-mile jog and stretching to as much as the pre-race warm-up: "It all depends on how I feel on that day."

FALL CROSS-COUNTRY TRAINING: Monday:8-10-mile run through aboretum. Tuesday: 10x880y slow with 2-3-minute interval, on grass. Wednesday: 8-10-mile run over hills. Thursday: 20x440y in 65 seconds with 2-minute interval. Friday: 8-10-mile run. Saturday: Fartlek or rest. Sunday: Rest.

WINTER TRAINING: Monday: 20x440y averaging 64.9 with 220y walk-jog interval, or 8x440y in 58.5 with 220y walk-jog. Tuesday: 10x220y in 27.3 with 110y walk, 5x300y in 36.0 with 140y walk-jog. Wednesday: 6x660y in 1:35.8 with 220y walk-jog. Thursday: 6-8 race pace 220y or 300y with 110y jog interval. Friday: Rest or pre-race warm-up. Saturday: Race 1000y and mile relay. Sunday: Easy jogging or rest.

SPRING/SUMMER TRAINING: Morning workouts during this period are easy 5-mile runs at 8 AM Monday through Thursday. Monday: 220y in 56.5 seconds, 220y in 26.0 seconds with 120y jog interval (except 220y jog before 660y), 1-2-miles of striding straightaways and jogging curves. Tuesday: 4-5x330y in 38-40 seconds with 150y walk, 8-10x150y accelerating to near full speed, 1-2 miles of striding straights and jogging curves. Wednesday: 4x550y, accelerating in last 110y (first 440y in 53 seconds) 2-3x330y at race pace, 6-8x150y at race pace or faster, 1-2 miles of striding straights and jogging curves. Thursday: 20x50y dashes at ¾ speed on grass with short interval, or 6-8x220y at race pace. Friday: Rest or pre-race warm-up. Saturday: Race. Sunday: 10-12-mile easy run along grassy, scenic route.

Winzenried clocked 47.8 for 440y as a high school junior, 1:50.9 for 880y as senior, and 1:46.5 for 800m as an 18-year-old college freshman. An aggressive competitor, he prefers to lead and set a quick pace. He does no weight training and rests 2-4 weeks between fall and winter training periods. He has been coached by Rut Walter, Bob Brennan, Dick Glendenning, and Stan Barr.

Mark has been one of America's top two-lap runners since 1968. He ran 1:45.6 in 1970 and ranked 5th in the world, placing 2nd in the AAU. He won the NCAA title in 1971 and ranked 10th in the world. In Feb. 1972, he lowered the indoor 1000 world record to 2:05.1 on Louisville's large track. He had a mile best in 1972, 3:59.5 and a 2:18.0 for 1000m.

Mark Winzenried

# Dave Wottle

DAVID JAMES WOTTLE, Bowling Green State University, Ohio. Age 19 years, 1969.

BEST MARKS: 6 miles, 30:55.5; 3 miles, 14:00.0; 2 miles, 8:58.8; mile, 3:59.0; 880y, 1:47.8; 440y, 50.2; 100y, 10.8(e).

PERSONAL STATISTICS: Born August 7, 1950 at Canton, Ohio. 6', 138 lbs. Started racing in 1965 at age 14.

PRE-RACE WARM-UP: Beginning 30 minutes before race, run 1 mile starting slowly and increasing pace to a relaxed 6:00 per mile.

PRE-TRAINING WARM-UP: 3-5 miles starting slowly, building to 6:30 pace, and finishing with final 880y about 2:30.

FALL CROSS-COUNTRY TRAINING: Monday: Mile in 5:15, 5 minute rest, 880y in 2:20 in 28 seconds, 2 minute rest, 440y in 70 seconds, 3 minute rest, 880y in 2:20, 5 minute rest, mile in 5:00, 2 mile jog. Tuesday: 20x440y in 70 seconds with 1 minute interval, 2 mile jog. Wednesday: 20 minute calisthenics, 4 mile time trial against teammates, 2 mile jog. Thursday: 8 mile fartlek averaging about 6:30 per mile. Friday: 2-3 miles easy running on golf course. Saturday: Race. Sunday: 10 mile run at 6:30 per mile. No morning workouts during this fall season.

WINTER TRAINING: Monday: 4-5 mile jog, 4x¾ mile in 3:20 with 440y walk-jog interval, 4 mile jog. Tuesday: 3-4 miles, 20x220y in 32 seconds with 220y jog, 5 miles. Wednesday: 4 miles, 6x880y in 2:05 with 440y walk interval, 4 miles. Thursday: 6 mile fartlek, 4x440y in 70 seconds + 60y full speed at end, 4x440y increasing tempo each 50y with 1 minute rest after each 440y, 4-5 miles. Friday: 5 miles, 1½ miles of alternating hard and easy 110's, 3-4 miles. Saturday: 12 mile jog. Sunday: 12 miles.

SPRING/SUMMER TRAINING: Two workouts per day are done during this period. Monday through Thursday mornings, runs of 7 miles at 6:30 pace are done at 7:15 AM. Monday: 4 miles, 2x2 miles in 9:48 and 9:30 with 20 minutes rest between, 3 mile jog. Tuesday: 3 miles, 19x440y (6 in 70 seconds, 4 in 68, 2 in 67, 2 in 66 and 1 each in 65, 64, 62, 60) with 220y walk after each. 2 mile jog. Wednesday: 3 miles, 1320y in 3:03, 880y in 2:03, 440y in 69 seconds with full recovery after each, racing with teammates; 3 mile jog. Thursday: 2 mile jog. Friday—AM, 4 miles at 7:00 pace. PM, 3-4 miles at 7:30 pace. Saturday—AM, 2-3 miles at 7:30 pace. PM, Race. Sunday: 12 mile run at 6:30 pace.

A 4:20.2 miler as a prep, Wottle improved to 4:06.8 as a college freshman. As a sophomore he was an NCAA All-American in both track and cross-country, and he won the USTFF 880y in 1:47.8. He competes in about 7 cross-country, 6 indoor, and 9 outdoor track races per year. He rests from training 5 weeks after cross-country and 4 weeks after outdoor track. Twice weekly he does light weight training. He has been coached by Everett Daniels and Melvin Brodt.

*Slowed by injuries in 1971, Dave Wottle came on strong in 1972. He won the King Games mile in 3:58.5, the NCAA 1500 in 3:39.7. A mistake in judgment cost him a chance to run in the Munich 1500 final. In the 800 though, Wottle was supreme. At the Olympic Trials in Eugene he equaled the world record with 1:44.3 and went on to become the Olympic champion in 1:45.9.*

Dave Wottle

# HOW THEY TRAIN
## 1500m./Mile

## Francesco Arese

FRANCO ARESE, Balangerco club, Italy. Age 25 years, 1969.

BEST MARKS: 10km, 28:27; 5000m., 13:40; 3000m., 7:51.2; 2000m., 5:03.4; mile, 3:56.7; 1500m., 3:36.3; 1000m., 2:16.9; 800m., 1:47.1 (all Italian records); 400m., 50.4.

PERSONAL STATISTICS: Born April 13, 1944 at Centalto, Italy. 6'1½'', 152 lbs. Started racing in 1961 at age 17.

DECEMBER—JANUARY TRAINING: Continuous runs 6-7 times per week at 7:10 per mile at first and at 6:10-6:25 by the end of January.

FEBRUARY TRAINING: 3 sessions a week at increased speed and other days the same as January.

COMPETITIVE SEASON TRAINING: Monday: 1 hour run and calisthenics. Tuesday: 10x400m. on track in 59 seconds, walk 2½-3 minutes after each. Wednesday: 1-1½ hours fartlek in park. Thursday: 6-8x600m. on track in 1:35, jog or walk 3-4 minutes after each. Friday: 40 minutes jog. Saturday: 10-15x200m. on track in 27-28 seconds, walk 2 minutes after each. Sunday: Light workout or rest.

*Although primarily a 1500m.-miler, Arese is a world class runner from 800m.-10,000m. Set 4 Italian records in 2 months in 1971. He was the 1970 European Cup and 1971 European Championship titlist at 1500m. Also ranked 2nd in the world at that distance in 1970. His 800m. best came in 1972, 1:46.6.*

## Sam Bair

SAMUEL PORTER BAIR, JR., Kent State University and Florida Track Club. Age 23, 1969.

BEST MARKS: 2-miles, 8:46.2; 1 mile, 3:58.7; 1500m., 3:41.4; ¾ mile, 2:58.7 (t); 880y, 1:50.2; 800m., 1:49.5; 440y, 49.7 (e); 220y, 23.6 (e); 100y, 10.4 (e).

PERSONAL STATISTICS: Born May 21, 1946 at Mt. Pleasant, Pennsylvania. 5'6¼", 124 lbs. Started racing in 1960 at age 14.

PRE-RACE WARM-UP: Jog 10-15 minutes. 10 minutes calisthenics. Jog another 10 minutes. 4x50y at ¾ full speed. Walk 30y after each. Then 3-5x100y at 7/8 full speed. Walk 50y after each. Then easy jogging and walking until 5 minutes before race.

PRE-TRAINING WARM-UP: Jog 1 mile. 5 minutes calisthenics. 3x50y at ¾ full speed, using exaggerated knee-lift. Walk 30y after each. Then 3x100y at 7/8 full speed. Walk 50y after each. No warm-up prior to long training runs.

FALL TRAINING: Monday—PM, 10 miles road run in 68 minutes. Tuesday— AM, 10 miles road run in 67 minutes. PM, 20x220y fast striding on golf course. Jog 150y after each. Then 10x100y fast striding. Walk 35-50y after each. Wednesday—AM, 10 miles road run in 67 minutes. PM, 8 miles road run in 55 minutes. Thursday—PM, 14 miles road run in 95 minutes. Friday—AM, 9 miles road run in 59 minutes. PM, 10 miles road run in 67 minutes. Saturday—AM, 9 miles road run in 57 minutes. PM, Training on golf course. Fast, relaxed running, but not timed. 5x660y, jog 660y after each. 12x440y, jog 440y after each. 10x100y, walk 35y after each. Sunday—PM, 17 miles road run in 115 minutes.

Sam Bair

WINTER TRAINING: Saturday, 3/8/69—AM, 8 miles road run in 54 minutes. Sunday, 3/9/69—PM, 6 miles road run in 45 minutes. Monday, 3/10/69—¾ mile in 2:59.5. Tuesday, 3/11/69—AM, 11 miles road run in 75 minutes. PM, 6x440y in 58-59 seconds. Jog 440y after each. Wednesday and Thursday 3/13-14/69—Rest. Friday—Won NCAA indoor mile in 4:01.7.

SPRING/SUMMER TRAINING: Monday—PM, 15 miles road run in 100 minutes. Tuesday—AM, 9 miles road run in 100 minutes. Sprinted 6 hills of 75-100y each enroute. PM, 4x440y in 58.5. Jog 440y after each. 4x220y in 27.3. Jog 220y after each. 4x440y in 58.5. Jog 440y after each. 16x110y at 7/8 full speed. Walk 60y after each. Wednesday—PM, 4x220y in 25-26 seconds each. Jog 220y after each. Terminated workout due to sore legs. Thursday—15 miles in 102 minutes on roads. Friday—Rest. Saturday—Competition. Mile in 4:10.8. 880y in 1:55.0. 3-miles in 15:00.

Uses weight training twice weekly. Jogs one mile warm-down after track workouts. Coached by Doug Raymond, Don Gilpin, Jerome Marco, & Harry Mehillik.

*Sam Bair's mile best came in 1969 when he finished second to Jim Ryun at Compton in 3:56.7.*


## Phil Banning

PHILIP ANDREW BANNING, Andover A.C. and Villanova. Age 19, 1969.

BEST MARKS: 15 miles, 1:30:00 (e); 10 miles, 57:00 (e); 6 miles, 29:40; 3 miles, 13:55; 2 miles, 8:46.5; 3000m., 8:16.7; 1½ miles, 6:41 (r); mile, 4:02.9; 1500m., 3:45.2; 1320y, 2:59; 1000m., 2:30; 1000y, 2:15 (e); 880y, 1:56.9; 800m., 1:53 (r); 660y, 1:23 (e); 440y, 53.2 (r); 330y, 37.5 (t); 220y, 24.8; 110y, 11.2.

PERSONAL STATISTICS: Born October 10, 1950 in Penton Grafton, England. 5'6½", 127 lbs. Started racing in 1965 at age 15.

PRE-RACE WARM-UP: Jog 2-3 miles. Stretching exercises. Stride and sprint 4-6x90-100y and then jog slowly till race.

PRE-TRAINING WARM-UP: Same as pre-race warm-up, but usually not done before long runs or during cross-country season. Jog until warm before cross-country.

FALL CROSS-COUNTRY TRAINING: Monday—AM, 5 miles in 35 minutes. PM, 10 miles in 70 minutes. Tuesday—AM, 5 miles in 35 minutes. PM, 10 miles in 70 minutes. Wednesday—AM, 5 miles in 35 minutes. PM, 10 miles in 70 minutes. Thursday—AM, 5 miles in 35 minutes. PM, 10 miles in 70 minutes. Friday—AM, 5 miles in 35 minutes. PM, Easy mile run. 3 mile run cross-country in 15 minutes. Rest. 5 miles in 30 minutes. Saturday—AM, 5 miles in 35 minutes. PM, 10 miles in 65 minutes. Sunday—AM, 5 miles in 35 minutes. PM, 10 miles in 65-70 minutes.

WINTER TRAINING: Monday—AM, 15 miles easy run. PM, 10 miles easy on golf course. Tuesday—PM, 30x440y in 68. Jog 440y in 2½ minutes after each. Last 440y in 58. Wednesday—AM, 10 miles in 70 minutes. PM, 12 miles. Thursday—AM, 5 miles in 35 minutes. PM, 10 miles on golf course in 60 minutes. Friday—PM, 10 miles run in 60 minutes. Saturday—AM, 3 miles cross-country race. PM, 6½ miles easy. Sunday—AM, 10 miles in 65 seconds.

SPRING/SUMMER TRAINING: Monday—AM, 16x110y. Jog 110y after each. Jog 2 miles. PM, 880y fast. Jog 440y. 2x660y, Jog 440y between. Jog 440y. 3x440y. Jog 220y between. Jog 440y. 4x330y. Walk 110y between. Jog 440y. 5x220y. Jog 220y between. Jog 440y. 6x110y. Jog 110y between. 2 mile warm-down. Tuesday—AM, 16x110y. Jog 110y between. Jog 2 miles. Tuesday—PM, 6x110y. Jog with 110y between. Jog 440y. 4x220y. Jog 220y between. 2x330y. Walk 110y between. Jog 440y. 1x440y. Jog 440y. 2x330y. Walk 110y between. Jog 440y. 4x220y. Jog 220y between. Jog 440y. 6x110y. Jog 110y between. Jog 2 miles. Wednesday—AM, 16x110y. Jog 110y jog between. 2 mile jog. PM, Swimming in afternoon. Later in evening, Weight workout: half squats, sit-ups, presses, military presses, overswings, bicep curls. Thursday—AM, 16x1106. Jog 110y between. Jog one mile. 10x110y up slight hill with jog 110y down hill after each. Jog 3 miles. PM, 2x220y. Jog 220 between. Jog 440y. 2x330y. Walk 110y between. Jog 440y. 2x440y. Jog 220y between. Jog 440. 1x660. Repeat pyramid backwards, finishing with 10x110y. Jog 110y between. Friday—AM, 4x550y. Walk 110y between. Jog 440y. 4x440y, Walk 110y between. Jog 440y. 4x330y. Walk 110y between. Jog 440. 4x220y. Walk 110y between. Jog 440y. 4x110y. Walk 110y between. Jog mile. PM, 16x100y. Jog 110y between. Jog mile. Saturday—Jog 440y. 11 miles cross-country run in 66 minutes. Jog 440y. Jog one mile. Weight workout: half squats, sit-ups, press-ups, military presses, overswings, bicep curls, step-ups. 5 miles cross-country easy. Sunday—1500m. race. Jog 3 miles. 10x110y. Jog 110y. Jog one mile.

Coached by John Mullen, Jumbo Elliot and Martin Andover. Participates in 8 indoor, 27 cross-country and 25 outdoor meets annually.

National Juniors mile champion in 1968. AAA Junior champion in 1500m. with 3:45.2.

## Roger Bannister

DR. ROGER GILBERT BANNISTER, Great Britain.

BEST MARKS: mile, 3:58.8; 1500m., 3:43.8; ¾ mile, 2:52.9t; 880, 1:50.7; 660, 1:20.2; 440, 51.0.

PERSONAL STATISTICS: Born March, 1929 in England. 6'2", 154 lbs. Started formal racing in 1946 at age 17 and retired in 1954 at age 25. Training in the fall 1946 at Exeter College, Oxford consisted of running once during the week and racing on Saturday. In the spring, track training was started.

1948 TRAINING: Run for ¾ hour, 3-4 days per week.

1949-1950 TRAINING: Alternating slow runs of 1¼ miles with faster runs of ½-¾ mile, 4 days per week. Later this was modified along the lines of fartlek.

1950-1952 TRAINING: Stepped up training program in the fall. In the spring trained 5 days a week with interval method.

1951-1952 TRAINING: Ran on grass for never longer than ½ hour after work, 3-4 days per week. Track training was begun in February.

1952-1953 TRAINING: Interval method was used as training was increased. In February and March track training was started, sometimes running as many as 10x440 in 63 seconds with 2-3 minutes rest after each.

1953-1954 TRAINING: Starting in December, ran 5 times a week during noon hour. Several days consisted of 10x440 in 66 seconds with a 2 minute rest after each. During the following months they were gradually speeded up till by the end of April the average had dropped to 59 seconds per 440. Following are some highlights of Bannister's training 3 weeks before his 3:59.4 world record: April 12—7x880 in 2:06. April 14—¾ mile in 3:02. April 15—½ mile in 1:53.0. April 22—10x440 in 58.9. April 24—¾ mile in 3:00.0. April 28—¾ mile in 2:59.9. April 30—½ mile in 1:54.0.

DURATION OF WORKOUT: 1 hour from 5-6 PM, 3-5 times a week. Raced not more than twice a month. It was his custom to run a ¾ mile time trial a few days before an important race. He preferred to follow in a race till he unleashed his kick in the final lap.

Bannister gained immortality on May 6, 1954 when he became the first man to crack the much sought after 4-minute mile (3:59.4). Another memorable race came on August 7, 1954 at Vancouver during the British Empire Games when he outkicked John Landy in a personal record, 3:58.8.

He was self-coached throughout his career. Because he kept experimenting with different training and racing methods, Bannister felt that only he could determine what training was best suited for him. However he did have some guidance from Franz Stampfl during his final year. Bannister always kept running, which gave him a deep feeling of satisfaction even from his childhood, but never let it affect his academic life. Because of this he never subscribed to the 7-day-a-week training regimen, and rarely trained 5 days a week till the last years of his career.

He was Oxford-Cambridge mile champion 1947-1950. He was also AAA champion in the mile in 1951, 1953, 1954 and half mile in 1952. In 1954 he became the British Empire Games mile and 1500m. European champion. He finished 4th in the 1952 Olympic 1500m. and was a member of the British 1953 world record 4-mile relay team.

Roger Bannister, after British Empire Games victory over John Landy in 3:58.8.

# Joe Binks

JOE BINKS, England. Age 84.

Established world record for mile in 1902 (4:16.8). This remained a British record for 20 years until broken by Albert Hill.

BEST MARKS: 3 mile, 14:10; mile, 4:16.8; 880, 1:56; 440, 50.0; 330, 31.0; 100, 10.6.

PERSONAL STATISTICS: Born in London. 142 lbs.

Raced 15 years in top class, and another 10 years in second class.

WARM-UP: "Never did any warm-up. Just did a couple of leg stretches (short runs) across the arena."

TRAINING: "I trained only one evening per week, winter and summer, spending about 30 minutes on each workout. My training would not be understood today. It was always light. In training for sprint races, I would run 5 or 6x60 to 110 yard bursts of speed and finish with a fast 220 or 300 yards. I trained the same for a mile or 880 yards race, doing several sprints, and 440 yards or 600 yards at varying pace, first part slow, middle part medium, and finish fast. In training for 3 miles, I ran 2 miles easily, then sprints. No time trials in training. I can hardly understand today's terrifically heavy training and racing—if it is that which has produced today's fast times (records), all I can say is they cannot last very long at it. Having discovered one can race fast from start to finish without resting or coasting explains these fast times today. In my day, one ran to a schedule, which looks easy today. "You will laugh at my 'slap dash' method of training, but I got a lot of fun out of it, which today's champions do not get." Participated in approximately 12 cross country and road races and "dozens" of track races annually . . . Was self-coached . . . Did no weight training . . . Binks became a world famous sports writer and athletics promoter with "News of the World" in London. It is difficult to describe the great good this athlete, sports promoter, and gentleman has done for athletics. "I was invariably bothered by stitch in side in cross country races. In the 1902 National 10-miles Cross Country Championship, I carried a small bottle of brandy. With 3 miles to go I was 52d. I finished 9th. I never tried that again."

# Dyrol Burleson

DYROL J. BURLESON, Cottage Grove (Oregon) High School. Age 18, 1958.

BEST MARKS: Mile, 4:12.2 and 4:13.2; 880, 1:54.0; 440, 51.7; 220, 24.3; 100, 11.0.

PERSONAL STATISTICS: Born April 27, 1940 at Cottage Grove, Oregon. 6'1", 157 lbs. Started racing in 1954, age 14.

RACE WARM-UP: 15-20 minutes fartlek (about 2 miles). 6-10 minutes calisthenics.

TRAINING WARM-UP: Jog 440. 10 minutes calisthenics. As a high school freshman, age 15, in 1955, Burleson ran a 4:43.2 mile and 2:11 880. His training consisted primarily of 3 miles fartlek twice per week, and 8-10x440 in 70-75, walking 440 after each on other days. As a 16 year old sophomore in 1956, he ran a 4:33.4 mile and 2:03 880. His training consisted of 3-4 miles fartlek once per week, and on other days 8-10x440 with a 440 walk after each. The speed of the 440's ranged from 68 seconds in early season to 62 seconds in late season. He also ran 220's in 34. As a junior in 1957, age, 17, Burleson ran a 4:24.4 mile and 1:57.3 880. His training consisted of 40 minutes fartlek (about 5 miles) once every 2 weeks. On other days he ran 8-10x440 at speeds ranging from 67 down to 64. In early season he walked 440's after each, and in late season he walked 220's. He also ran repeat 220's in 28 to 33. On April 25, 1958 Burleson established a national high school mile record of 4:13.2 at the Corvallis Invitational Meet. (61, 64, 66, 62.2).

1958 PRE-COMPETITIVE SEASON TRAINING: Monday: (2/24/58) 10-12x440 in 68. Jog 440's. Tuesday: (2/25/58) 5-7x660 in 1:45. Jog 440's. Wednesday: (2/26/58) 10-14x220 in 33. Jog 440's Then light fartlek, briefly. Thursday: (2/27/58) 5-8x880 in 2:16. Jog 440's. Friday: (2/28/58) 4-6x440 in 68. Jog 440's. 8-10x220 in 33. Jog 220's. Fartlek. Saturday: (3/1/58) 20 minutes fartlek (about 3 miles). Sunday: (3/2/58) 1 hour fartlek on golf course.

MID-COMPETITIVE SEASON TRAINING: Saturday: 4/19/58: 880 in 1:58.3 and 440 in 52.3. Sunday 4/20/58: 20 minutes fartlek. Monday 4/21/58: 16-24x220 in 31. Jog 220's. Light fartlek. Tuesday 4/22/58: 10-12x440 in 64. Jog 220's. Wednesday 4/23/58: 440 in 64, jog 220. 880 in 2:08, jog 220. 440 in 64. Light fartlek. Thursday 4/24/58: Rest. Friday 4/25/58: Mile in 4:13.2. 880 in 2:02.1.

Above workouts followed by warm down of light jogging for about 1 mile.

Prior to 1958, Burleson ran the first 440 of his miles races too fast. He attempts to run his races at a steady, even pace. He ran cross-country from 9/1/57 to mid-November, 1957 (12 cross-country races). From mid-November, 1957, to January 1, 1958, he took two workouts weekly. He started daily training 1/1/58, and his track season ended in mid-June, 1958. Ran 12 outdoor track meets, frequently running both mile and 880 in same meet. Coached by Wallace Ciochetti in 1955 and 1956, and by Sam Bell in 1957 and 1958. His 4:12.2 mile came after graduation from high school, in the national AAU. His workouts are started at 2:15 PM. Each training session is 1 to 2 hours duration, the average being somewhere near 1½ hours. Often he runs fartlek in the evening twilight, in addition to his daily training.

*After high school, Burleson went on to the University of Oregon and for several years was one of America's top milers. He competed in two Olympic Games (6th in 1960, 5th in 1964), was ranked first in the world in 1961, 2nd in 1963. His best mile was 3:55.6, his best 1500 was 3:38.8.*

Dyrol Burleson

# Jim Crawford

JAMES B. CRAWFORD, U.S. Army. Age 24 years. 1971.

BEST MARKS: 18 miles, 1:47:00; 15 miles, 1:20:00; 10 miles, 50:05; 10km, 30:59.2; 6 miles, 29:58; 3 miles, 13:38.6; 2 miles, 8:54.4; mile, 3:57.7; 1500m., 3:43.0; ¾ mile, 2:57.0; 880, 1:51.0; 660, 1:21.0; 440, 48.8r; 330, 36.0; 220, 23.0; 100, 10.7.

PERSONAL STATISTICS: August 17, 1947 at Hackensack, New Jersey. 5'7", 130 lbs. Started racing in 1962 at age 15.

PRE-RACE WARM-UP: Jog 2-3 miles, stretching, 2-4x150 hard then walk and keep loose till race.

PRE-TRAINING WARM-UP: Jog 2 miles easy.

FALL CROSS-COUNTRY TRAINING: Monday: 20 miles in 2 hours. Tuesday—AM, 8½ miles. PM, 6½ miles. Wednesday: 20½ miles in 2:05. Thursday: 15½ miles in 1½ hours. Friday: Easy 15 miles in 1:44. Saturday—AM, 11½ miles. PM, 12½ miles. Sunday: 20 miles.

WINTER TRAINING: Monday—AM, 3 miles in 18 minutes. PM, 5xmile ave. 4:32.8 on roads, jog 3 minutes after each. Tuesday—AM, 3 miles in 21 minutes. PM, 11 miles. Wednesday—AM, 3 miles. PM, 16x330 ave. 46.2 on grass with 330 jog after each. Thursday—AM, 4 miles. PM, 11 miles. Friday—AM, 3 miles. PM, 3x2 miles ave. 9:32 on roads with 4 minute jog after each, 1½ mile jog, stride ½ mile in 2:30. Saturday—AM, 11 miles. PM, 4 miles. Sunday—AM, 4 miles in 25 minutes. PM, 9 miles.

SUMMER TRAINING: Monday—AM, 6 miles, PM, 4x220 ave. 27.7, jog 220 after each, 3x330 ave. 41.8, walk 110 after each, 440 in 54.5, 3x330 ave. 43.3, walk 110 after each, 4x220 ave. 28.1, jog 220 after each, jog 440 after each series. Tuesday—AM, 6 miles. PM, 18 miles in 1:49. Wednesday—AM, 3 miles to park, 20 minutes fartlek, 3 miles back from park. PM, 2 miles to beach, 10x700 striding in the surf with 15 seconds rest after each, 2 miles back from beach. Thursday—AM, 7 miles. PM, 880 in 1:54.7, 660 in 1:25.8, 440 in 53.5, 330 in 39.0, jog 880 after each run. Friday—AM. Same as Wednesday. PM, 7 miles. Saturday: 15 miles in 1:23. Sunday—AM, 7 miles. PM, 8x880, odd number runs ave. 2:01, even number runs ave. 2:12.1, on the roads with 45-second rest after each.

Duration of workouts: 45-50 minutes at 8 AM and 1½-2 hours at 4 PM. Participates in 1 cross-country, 6 indoor, and 12 outdoor races per year. Prefers to follow and sprint hard the last 250 yards. He usually lifts weights every day during fall and winter. Crawford won the 1968 USTFF mile and the 1969 NAIA indoor mile. He holds Arkansas Intercollegiate Conference records in the 2 mile, mile, and 880. He also holds Arkansas college state records in the 6 mile, 3 mile,

2 mile, mile, and 1500m. Has been coached by Larry Smith, Ted Lloyd, Ralph Higgins, and the late Dr. Robert T. Clark. He credits the guidance of Gordon Scoles with his most recent success and progress. *Crawford's bests came down to 3:40.3 (1500) and 8:36.0 (2 miles) in 1972.*

Glenn Cunningham

# Glenn Cunningham

GLENN CUNNINGHAM, University of Kansas and New York Curb Exchange A.A.

BEST MARKS: 2 mile, 9:11.8; mile, 4:04.4 (indoors, 1938), 4:06.7 (world record outdoors, 1934); 1500m, 3:48.0; ¾ mile, 3:00.8; 1000, 2:10.1 (world record indoors, 1935); 800m, 1:49.7 (world record, 1936); 600, 1:11.3 (world record indoors, 1938); 440, 47.2; 100, 10.2.

PERSONAL STATISTICS: Born in 1907 in Kansas. 5'9", 165 lbs. First received national publicity with 4:24.7 interscholastic mile record in 1930. Ended racing career in 1940 at age 33.

WARM-UP: 1½-2 miles in sweat suit and heavy soled basketball shoes.

PRE-COMPETITIVE SEASON TRAINING: "I ran longer distances in the fall, between 2 to 6 or 8 miles each night. If I ran longer distances (6-8 miles) it was slower, but always a good tough workout finished off with a 100 yard sprint. I paid no attention to time during this 8 to 10 week period. Then I started pace and speed work, with no attention to distance. I would begin with a 2 miles warm-up wearing heavy basketball shoes and sweat clothes, between 9:30 and 10:30. I have run 9:17 for a 2 miles warm-up. On one day I would run 2x660, and walk 880 after each, followed by short sprints. Another day it would be 3x440, walking 440 yards after each, followed by a short sprint. 2 or 3 times during the season a ¾ mile, and an occasional 880. I never ran the mile for time."

COMPETITIVE SEASON TRAINING: (Each warm-up of 2 miles in 9:30 to 10:30.) Monday: "A few sharp sprints." Tuesday: 3x440 in 55-58. Walk 440's. Or, 2x660 in 1:25-1:29. Walk 880 between. Wednesday: "A few 50-100 yard sprints." Thursday: Warm-up. Friday: Rest. Saturday: Race. Sunday: Leisurely walk. "If I found in a race I was short on endurance, I'd work harder on the warm-up early in the week and go faster on the sprints. Occasionally I would run ¾ mile in 2:20-2:30 for the first 880, and then finish with a 58 or 60 second 440. In all my running I tried to concentrate on form and relaxation. Proper relaxation makes possible recuperation while running, I think. Pace judgment is important, and you must work on it constantly until mastered. Rest is as important as work." Cunningham's legs were badly burned in a schoolhouse fire at Elkhart, Kansas. Amputation seemed necessary. Somehow the scarred tissues healed. At age 8 he took up running to strengthen his legs. It is estimated that during his great career the mighty Kansan ran in excess of 10,000 miles including training. He was to indoor track in America what Babe Ruth was to baseball and Bill Tilden was to tennis, a colorful and tremendous competitor who brought out great crowds wherever he appeared. He represented the USA in 1500m at two Olympics, placing 2d in 1936. Cunningham is truly one of the most magnificent and glamorous runners in American track history.

## Ron Delany

RONALD MICHAEL DELANY, Villanova University and Crusaders A.C., Dublin. Age 23, 1958.

BEST MARKS: Mile, 3:57.5; 880, 1:47.8.

PERSONAL STATISTICS: Born March 6, 1935 at Arklow, Ireland. 6', 146 lbs. Started racing in 1951 at age 16.

WARM-UP: Jog 15 minutes. 5 minutes calisthenics. Alternately stride 100-150 yards and walk 100-150 yards. Then go directly into workout or rest 30 minutes prior to race.

WINTER TRAINING: Monday: 7½ miles cross country run. Tuesday: 10x440 in 61.5 average. Jog 440 after each. Wednesday: 5 miles road run. Thursday: 5 miles continuous running on board track. Friday: Rest. Saturday: Mile race. Sunday: Rest.

TRAINING DURING OUTDOOR TRACK SEASON: Monday: 5 miles fast cross country run. Tuesday: 10x440 in 60 or faster. Jog 440 after each. Wednesday: 20x220 in 27.5 average. Jog 220 after each. Thursday: 4 miles easy continuous running. Friday: Rest. Saturday: Race. Sunday: Fartlek running for one hour on grass.

STRATEGY: Follow and win with kick.

Ron Delany          Gianni Del Buono

DURATION OF WORKOUT: One hour, starting at 4:00 PM.

Participated each weekend, January through June annually, while representing Villanova. 1956 Olympic 1500m champion in 3:41.2. Holder of numerous NCAA, IC4A, and AAU titles. No special eating habits. In 1958 NCAA meet ran all-time fastest double of 4:03.5 mile and 1:48.6 880 . . . Established world indoor mark in 1958 at 4:03.4. Coached by Jack Sweeney, Louis Vandendries, and Jim (Jumbo) Elliott.

## Gianni Del Buono

GIOVANNI DEL BUONO, Istituto Superiore Educazione Fisica, in Urbano, and Cus Roma club in Rome. Age 26, 1969.

BEST MARKS: 3000m, 8:18.6; 2000m, 5:16.5, mile, 4:04.7; 1500m, 3:40.5; 1000m, 2:20.5; 800m, 1:48.3; 600m, 1:17 (e).

PERSONAL STATISTICS: Born October 4, 1943 in Ancona. 5'11", 143 lbs. Started racing in 1959 at age 16.

PRE-RACE WARM-UP: 30-35 minutes of running at 4:40 mile pace. 10-15 minutes of calisthenics. 20-25 minutes of 100-150m windsprints with no fixed recovery. 10-15 minutes of slow running.

PRE-TRAINING WARM-UP: 2x1000m at 5:30 per 1000m. 2x1000m at 5:00. 2x1000m at 4:40 per 1000m.

FALL CROSS-COUNTRY TRAINING: Monday: 60-70 minutes running on roads at 4:20 per kilometer. Tuesday: 20 minutes running at 4:40 per kilometer, then weight work. Wednesday: 20 minutes running at 4:20 per kilometer. 35-40 minutes running at 4:20 per kilometer. 20 minutes running at 4:25-4:30 per kilometer. Thursday: 60-70 minutes running at 4:15-4:20 per kilometer on roads. Friday: 30 minutes running at 4:20 kilometer pace on roads. 30-35 minutes running at 4:20 kilometer pace on a slope. 20 minutes running at 4:20 kilometer pace on roads. Saturday: 1 hour of running at 4:15-4:20 kilometer pace on roads. Sunday: Rest OR cross-country race.

WINTER TRAINING: Similar to cross-country training.

SPRING-SUMMER TRAINING: Monday: 30 minutes running at 4:30 per kilometer pace on grass. 10x100m in 15 seconds on grass. 15 minutes running at 4:30 per kilometer pace. Tuesday: 30 minutes running at 4:10 per kilometer pace on grass. 10x300 in 43-45. 20 minutes running at 4:40 per kilometer. Wednesday: 60 minutes fartlek. 30-45 minutes swimming. Thursday: 30 minutes running at 4:30 per kilometer pace on grass. 8-10x400m in 102 to 106 seconds with 400m recovery. Friday: 30 minutes running at 4:30 per kilometer on grass. 10-15x100m in 14.5. 4x200m in 26-27. Saturday: 30-40 minutes easy running. 10x100m in 13.5. Sunday: 30-40 minutes easy running.

Coached by D. Barletta and R. Funiciello. Participates in 4-6 cross-country, 1-2 indoor and 15-20 outdoor meets per year. Set Italian record in 800m in 1968 at 1:48.3. Ran on Italian record-setting 3200m. and 6000m. relay teams.

*In 1970 Del Buono improved to 3:39.3 and 4:00.3. Just after the 1972 Olympics where he failed to get past the first round in the 1500, Del Buono cracked the Italian 5000m. record with a 13:22.4 in Rome, a mark superior to the winning 5000m. time in Munich. In the race, he defeated Steve Prefontaine and Juha Vaatainen. He also had a world-leading 5:00.0 2000m. and a 7:49.4 3000m. after the Games.*

# Herb Elliott

HERBERT JAMES ELLIOTT, Aquinas College, Perth, Australia. Age 20, 1958.

BEST MARKS: 2 mile, 8:37.6; mile, 3:54.5 (WR); 1500m., 3:36.0 (WR); 880, 1:47.3.

PERSONAL STATISTICS: Born February 25, 1938 at Perth, Western Australia. 5'10½", 147 lbs. Started racing in 1953 at age 16. At age 17 he ran 1:55.7 and 4:20.4. At age 18 he ran 9:01.2, 4:04.4, 3:47.8, and 1:50.8. Two weeks after his 19th birthday he ran 4:00.4 and 1:49.0.

TRAINING: Herb Elliott does very little training on the track. He runs ten miles daily during the week in the parks of Melbourne. On weekends Herb motors 60 miles to Portsea, a rough seashore training camp owned by his coach, the controversial and unorthodox 64-year-old Percy Wells Cerutty. During these weekends at Portsea, Herb runs tremendous workouts, both in quantity and quality, along the beach, over a rough mile and a quarter long bush circuit with sandy surface, on a golf course, and up an 80 foot sandhill with a grade of two in one. Much of his running is continuous. He runs primarily according to how he feels, usually feels like running fast, and his slow running is only relatively slow. He calls his training over sandy surfaces "resistance running." Herb prefers his food raw. His favorite breakfast is uncooked rolled oats mixed with wheat germ, walnuts, and chopped fruit such as bananas, dried figs, dates, and raisins. Herb feels all of his sacrifices for the sake of training (such as no sugar in his tea) will be repaid in terms of greater athletic performances. He claims to have little idea of pace during a race, and feels that he could run a mile under four minutes twice a week indefinitely. He has acquired much of his philosophy of life from Cerutty, but he never hesitates to differ, and is almost as fit mentally as physically.

Herb Elliott is truly a fantastic physical speciman, not only through God-given natural ability, but as a result of unbelievably severe training wherein he figuratively runs himself to exhaustion. He fears no man in a track suit. He is a powerful surf swimmer, and in 1958 used this ability to save the life of his friend and teacher, Percy Cerutty, as Cerutty was caught in a fierce undertow beyond a rock shelf and swept into a maelstrom at Portsea beach.

The Australian track writer, Joe Galli, has described a weekend with Elliott at Portsea. "Arrived Saturday afternoon. Elliott and two friends had just returned from a 30 mile hike over the rugged terrain, sleeping under the stars at night. A day previously Herb had run a mile in four minutes. We dived into bunks at Cerutty's headquarters and slept nine hours. At 5:00 AM we were up. We jogged half a mile to the beach, spent 30 minutes running along the hard sand and plunging into the surf, then back for breakfast. Soon we were off again, running over a sandy, bush track course of just over a mile with two killing climbs. I was proud to break ten minutes for the course. Herb ran it five times, never in more than 6:10. Next—weight lifting. Elliott lifted 200 pounds in the ordinary dead lift, and 125 in the press. Lunch was followed by a discussion of training. Then we tackled a giant 80 foot sandhill. One run up the hill finished me. I found it even hard to walk through its deep loose sand. Elliott scampers up as though it were a moderate grass slope." *(World Sports,* Country and Sporting Publications Ltd., London, Nov., 1958, page 6, and July, 1958, page 8.)

After spending a weekend with Elliott and Cerutty at Portsea in November, 1958, Joe Galli wrote again: "Herb is stronger than last summer. On Sunday morning Elliott ran 15 miles along the Nepean highway. As usual, Herb scooted around the bush trails, heaved weights, surfed, and sun-baked on the beach. The rule at Portsea weekends (Friday night through Monday morning) is a complete break from city living. In warm weather (as now) the Cerutty men go barefooted for the weekend clad only in shorts. They don't shave, their bath is the ocean, and they eat huge quantities of plain, largely uncooked food, and work like demons." *(Athletics Weekly,* World Athletic and Sporting Publications, Ltd., Chatham, England, Vol. 12, No. 48, page 13, 11/29/58.)

Another observer described Elliott's training thusly: "After an early morning 14 mile run down a sandy road, round and round the rolling Portsea Golf Course, Elliott sprinted a final 100 yards and slumped to the sand. Catching his breath, he kicked off his trunks and mouldy shoes, and plunged into the frigid waters of Bass Strait. Then to an 80 foot sand dune over which he sprinted and continued through scrub and roots, over barbed wire fences to a clap-board ski-hut, into a cold shower, and to bed for 30 minutes of sound sleep. Then a meal of raw carrots, cabbage, brown broad, cheese and milk. Next, weight lifting with heavy barbells and heavy slabs of rail. This Saturday morning workout was only the beginning of two grinding days of running and exercising at a fitness fanatic's homemade commando course. For four days during the week, resting only on

Friday, Elliott had lifted weights and run ten miles daily in Melbourne's parks. He would run 50 miles during the weekend at Portsea, before shaving and returning to Melbourne. Elliott trains his hardest in off season, and during track season relaxes, races, and does a little jogging." *(Sports Illustrated,* New York, NY, Nov. 10, 1958, page 16.)

Much has been written about the feats of Elliott and the philosophy advocated by his coach, Percy Wells Cerutty. However, little specific information concerning Elliott's actual training techniques has reached print. The following (sometimes conflicting) advice advocated by Cerutty has been gleaned from numerous sources. According to Cerutty, civilized man is unfit because he has forgotten that running is an exercise carried out continuously by man in his natural state. He says to train as nature tells you. Don't be a slave to a stop watch. Run fast when you feel like it, not when a schedule tells you. Cerutty preaches manliness and the glory of defying pain. It is a joy through strength doctrine. He orders his athletes to be contemptuous of pain and thrust against it. He aimed to fashion a raw Elliott into a resilient, superbly conditioned, free spirit who would discipline himself instinctively and soar above the common herd of racers by virtue of superior strength and will power. Cerutty is embittered by the alleged rejection of his theories by Australian officials. Much of his coaching dogma is based on sheer emotion. What he advocates frequently diametrically opposes in bitter terms the methods adfocated by his coaching rivals, particularly Franz Stampfl, coach of Merv Lincoln and others, and a believer in "scientific" training methods.

Cerutty is a weight enthusiast, and advocates lifting very heavy weights (one half to two times body weight in dead lift). He also advocates running in knee-deep water or snow, and fast walking carrying heavy packs up steep mountains (climbs of from 3000 to 5000 feet in two to four hours). He believes the athlete must be built up to become a "front runner" (like Zatopek, Kuts, Landy, and Elliott). He feels most of us are capable of running fast enough for world records, but the problem is running far enough at a fast speed.

"Condition yourself over at least three years," says Cerutty. "Become really strong all over. Train three days a week to exhaustion, rest or run easier on the others. Run a lot of the speed you would race at—say the 60 second quarter, or a little faster. Run 220's, 440's, even 880's, and an occasional three-quarter mile. Get the organism drilled to running at these speeds and flat out until exhausted. Reduce the recovery times to a mere nothing as the intensive training goes on. Run a lot of over-distance work for continuity of effort. The times will come." *(Athletics Review,* The Hotspur Publishing Company, Manchester, England, Vol. 9, No. 6, Oct., 1955, page 9.)

"Conditioning applies to all distances from the sprints to six miles, but must be adapted to suit the individual's needs as well as his events. The sprinter needs to cover about 12-20 miles per week. The 440-880 man about 20-30 miles per week. The 880- one miler at least 40 miles weekly, perhaps more. The one miler-six miler also around 50 miles per week, but can do up to 100 sometimes. The marathon men need at least 300 miles per month. Half the work needs to be run at fast paces, with high knee lift, and strong vigorous stride, and the most vigorous arm and shoulder movement you are capable of. Do a mile or two of this, vary it with 440 yards slow, working into fast hard effort for 30, 50 or up to even 200 yards, then rest a bit by gentle jogging, pick up the hard slow work into another burst, and so on until tired. Once or twice a week do a good steady straight run of two miles for sprinters to ten miles for three and six milers. Once a month at least visit sand hills or very steep grass hills, and run up as hard as possible, walk down, and keep repeating until nearly dead. Also run on heavy, loose sand or the tan of a race course. This can be done each week. Twice a week work with heavy weights. Try to get four good sessions of training in each weekend, Saturday morning as well as races in afternoon. It is not justified to save yourself for more than two races in cross country season. Time is too valuable to waste on cross country if you wish to succeed in a big way. Give up all other hobbies other than your work and training. There is no room for any more if you do not want to see others get ahead of you. Live your athletics all the time. Every time you move or even sit you can practice running motions. Train all day. Eat only natural (uncooked) foods as much as possible. Make flaked oatmeal with raisins, honey, and walnuts a big part of each day's daily intake. Never drink water with or after meals. Drink plentifully not less than two hours after eating, and within 3 minutes or 10 minutes before a meal. Never eat between meals. Drink milk with meals. It is a solid. Eat crude medical molasses, malt extract or malt, cod-liver oil, wheat germ, one pound of fresh fruit daily, coarse wholewheat bread, raw vegetables, and vitamins. Get eight hours of sleep each night, preferably nine hours. There is no room for late hours in the life of a champion.

Herb Elliott

Asked why he runs, Herb Elliott said he regards it as a way of expressing himself through pain, and proving himself the better man. His tremendous physical and mental ability permits him to win with any strategy and tactic he chooses. He will lead throughout, win on the final sprint, or (most devastating of all), blast the entire final 600 yards of his mile.

*Elliott won the 1960 Olympic 1500 meters at Rome with a world record 3:35.6. He was never beaten in a mile race during his career.*


## Chris Fisher

CHRISTOPHER FISHER, Port Adelaide (Australia) A.C. Age 19, 1968.

BEST MARKS: 10 miles, 53:00; 1,500m., 3:45.1; 1 mile, 4:03:03; 1,200m., 2:54 (e); ¾ mile, 2:55 (e); 800m, 1:47 (e); 800, 1:48.4; 600m, 1:25; 660, 1:25; 400m, 49.5; 440, 50 (e); 300 yards, 33 (e); 200m, 23.5; 220, 23.8 (e); 100m, 11.5, 100, 10.6.

PERSONAL STATISTICS: Born October 2, 1949 at Renmark, South Australia. 6'0", 146 lbs. Started racing in 1966 at age 16.

PRE-RACE WARM-UP: 2 miles in 20 minutes, running around the outside of the track for 3 or 4 laps, then move onto the track for about 4-5 strides down the backstraight at ¾ top pace, then stretching exercises for about 3 minutes. Then, the race.

PRE-TRAINING; 1-½ miles in 10 minutes. Jog in a group of about 6 to 8 athletes who will all do the particular workout for the 4-6 laps, then a few stretching exercises to ensure not to pull a muscle. Then into the workout.

FALL CROSS-COUNTRY TRAINING: Monday—PM (5:30), Ten miles at good race pace with the emphasis on running relaxed and smoothly at all times. This takes place anywhere around Adelaide's outskirts at a 5:30 to 5:50 pace. Tuesday—PM (5:30), Fartlek around a golf course depending on how I feel as to how hard I run this particular workout. I am usually quite tired when I finish. Wednesday—PM (5:30), Speed work from Western District clubhouse in town. It varies quite a bit from 440's, 330's and 220's. Either 8x440 in 60-64, with 440 jog recovery (relaxed running speed) 12x330 in 44-48 or 15-20x220 in 27-30. Thursday—PM (5:30), Run about 2 miles to golf course and use that as a warm-up for the workout which consists of 30 sprints up hill on grass in bare feet. The hill is about 50 yards long and quite steep. This is a very hard workout. Friday—If I intend running a race the following day, I either do nothing at all or run a few miles on the grass, concentrating on form and relaxation and limbering up in general. Saturday—Sometimes compete in a cross-country race, usually title races only.

The idea is for training mainly. Usually 5 to 10 milers. Sunday—I go for an easy long run through Australia bush country in a National Reserve or along the many fine beaches of South Australia. About 6-8 of us go for a 15-20 mile run on Sunday morning at a 6-7 minute per mile pace.

WINTER TRAINING: Monday—PM (5:30), Usually run quite a solid fast 10 miles in a group around the outskirts of Adelaide. It is probably the hardest distance run for the week, approximately 54 minutes. Tuesday—I usually don't train in the mornings as time is usually quite limited. 5:30 PM, Speed work. I usually run 15x220 yards in 27-29 (¾ top pace) with 220 recovery or 12x330 (2/3 pace) with a 110 recovery. Wednesday—Fartlek over a golf course, usually sprinting up the hills and recovering on the downhill. This is done just as I feel, depending on the night. Sometimes it is very hard. Other times quite easy. Thursday—PM, (5:30), Sometimes I go straight home from work and run from my home. I have devised a good hard, hilly 5 mile course on the road which is quite testing. Friday—Train from the local clubshed in town and we set off for an easy 8 miles around the parklands of Adelaide (6:30 pace) which is most enjoyable. Saturday—Sometimes I compete in the local cross-country races, mainly for training, otherwise I do almost anything depending on what is organized. Usually another 5-6 mile run, relaxed. Sunday—AM (9-10), We go for a long run (10-15 miles, maybe more) along the beach or through National Park on all the brush tracks. We just run for about an hour and a half.

SPRING/SUMMER TRACK RACING SEASON: Monday—PM (5:30), Train with my personal coach when I run track work. Sometimes 1x880, then 10 minutes recovery, 1x660, 6 minutes recovery, 1x440, jog 440 recovery, 1x330, jog 2 laps, 1x220, 440 recovery, 5x110 sprints, all at top pace without straining. Tuesday—PM (5:30), Fartlek on the golf course from town. About 5 miles of changing pace. Sprinting up the hills and jogging back down as recovery. Wednesday—PM (5:30), Speed work, which (consists of 5x440 7/8 full pace) 440 jog recovery. Rest 10-15 minutes. Then 8x330 at fast striding pace with about 440 recovery. (40-43). Thursday—PM (5:30), I usually run in a group and do whatever I feel like running. Sometimes I run around the race course, which is 1-½ miles around. About 4 hard laps, then 110 sprints. Friday—Rest before competition next day. Saturday—Competition, Interclub. I run doubles sometimes early in the season for training, but mainly concentrate on one event and try to run a good time. Usually the 1,500 or 800 meters. Sunday—Early in the morning I go down to training and run through the water at knee depth. The frolic around and the weather make me enjoy myself.

STRATEGY: "Depends entirely on who I am running against and of how much importance the particular race is. I am not at all afraid to lead and set up the race if I think I can win by doing so. Also, I can 'sit' on someone and wait until the right time to kick for home."

On weight training: "Up to now I have not used weights but do intend to use them moderately in the future. Weights of about 80 lbs. (10-15 repetitions.)" Rests one day before competition, waits three hours between last meal and competition. George Govier has been his coach for the last three years. Participates in 24 outdoor and 6 cross-country races annually. Australian Junior 800 meters champion. South Australian Senior 1,500 meters record holder. Australian Junior 1,500 meters, steeplechase record holder and numerous junior state titles and records.

*Chris Fisher's best 800 dropped to 1:47.7 at the Commonwealth Games in 1970. He also had at 3:41.9 the same year. He came down to 1:47.0 and 3:39.5 the next year. In 1972, he also ran a 3:59.1 mile.*

## Gunder Hägg

GUNDER HÄGG, Kalarne Sports Club, Sweden.

BEST MARKS: 5000m, 13:58.2; 3 mile, 13:32.4; 2mile, 8:42.8; 2000m, 5:11.8; mile, 4:01.3; 1500m, 3:43.0 (all world records). 800m, 1:52.4.

PERSONAL STATISTICS: Born December 31, 1919 at Albacken, Sweden. 6', 150 lbs. Started racing in 1936 at age 17. Terminated racing career in 1945 at age 26.

PRE-RACE WARM-UP: Varied from almost nothing in hot weather to approximately 2000m. light running plus a brief, very warm shower in cold weather.

TRAINING: In his book entitled "Gunder Hägg's Diary", Hägg describes his training as follows: While doing military service in the far north of Sweden, he ran over the following 5000m. forest path daily from December, 1939, through the spring of 1940. Often in winter, Hägg had to fight with both arms and legs through huge snowdrifts to complete the course, frequently in temperatures much below zero (C). These were continuous runs, and he was extremely fatigued after each. A considerable amount of skiing and military marching was also included in his training. 1941 found Hägg residing at Valadalen, the famous resort hotel operated by Swedish sports enthusiast Gosta Olander. Hägg walked in deep snow, took long ski hikes (15-30Km), and ran over the following 5000m. forest path once or twice daily whenever possible.

The following specific workouts are noted in "Gunder Hägg's Diary":
April 21, 24, & 25, 1941: 6 Km. fast road run. April 22 and 26, 1941: 6 Km. moderate speed road run. April 23 and 28, 1941: 6 Km. alternately sprinting and jogging on road. 4/15/42: 3 Km. running in deep snow. 2 Km.

running on track. 4/16/42: 5 Km. light running on road and in woods. April 21, 22, and 23, 1942: 5 Km. alternately sprinting and easy running in woods. 4/30/43: Morning: 5 Km. sprinting and easy running. Evening: 6 Km. of same. 5/1/43: AM: 5 Km. light running on track. PM: 5 Km. sprinting and light running (track). 5/2/43: Morning: 5 Km. light running on track. Evening: Swedish bath. 5/3/43: Morning: 5 Km. sprinting and easy running. Evening: same. 5/4/43: 5 Km. light running on track. 5/5/43: 4 Km. sprinting and jogging. 5/23/45: Morning: 4 Km. fast running. Evening: same. May 24, 25, 27, & 28, 1045: AM: 4 Km. fast running. PM: 5 Km. alternately sprinting and light running.

Hägg raced hard and often throughout his career. During the summer of 1942 he established ten world records in seven different events within 82 days. He could lead or follow with equal success in his races. Hägg is regarded by many as the greatest middle distance runner the world has ever known.

## Arne Hamarsland

ARNE HAMARSLAND, Gular Club, Bergen, Norway. Age 26, 1959.

BEST MARKS: 10,000m., 30:43.4; 5000m., 14:35.8; 3000m., 8:13.2; mile, 4:00.8; 1500m., 3:39.8; 1000m., 2:20.0; 800m., 1:49.1; 400m., 50.1; 200m., 23.9; 100m. 11.6 seconds.

PERSONAL STATISTICS: Born July 24, 1933 at Bergen, Norway. Started racing in 1951 at age 17.

PRE-RACE WARM-UP: 15 minutes easy jogging mixed with 3-5x50-100m. of fast running during latter part. 10 minutes calisthenics. Walk 5-10 minutes. 3-6x150m. fast running in spikeshoes. Jog an equal distance after each. Duration of warm-up is 45 minutes, and preferably on grass.

PRE-TRAINING WARM-UP: 10-15 minutes fast jogging, followed by 5-10 minutes calisthenics.

WINTER TRAINING: January and February. On roads in extremely cold weather. Times approximate. No stop watch used. Sunday: 2-3 hours running and walking in woods or mountains, covering 10 to 20 miles. Monday: 10x150m. uphill sprints. Jog downhill in 75 to 90 seconds for recovery. Walk 5 minutes. 5x200m. in 28-30 seconds effort. Jog 200m. in 75 to 90 seconds after each. Tuesday and Friday: 10 miles speed play (fartlek). Included in this 10 miles are 8x200m. in 30-32 seconds effort and 8x400m. in 66-68 seconds effort. Jog 100-200m. in 45-60 seconds after each. Wednesday and Saturday: Rest. Thursday: 3x(5x200m. in

28-30 seconds effort. Jog 75 seconds after each. Walk 5 minutes after each series of 5x200m.).

PRE-COMPETITIVE SEASON TRAINING (April-May): Sunday: 60 minutes jogging in woods. Monday: On track. 5x400m. in 60-61 seconds each. Jog 400m. in 2½ minutes after each. Walk 5 minutes. 10x150m. in 20 seconds each. Jog 75 seconds recovery after each. Tuesday: 10x200m. at 27-28 seconds effort, on slightly uphill grass surface. Jog 200m. in 90 seconds after each. Wednesday and Saturday: Rest. Thursday: 12x400m. in 64 seconds each. Jog 400m. in 2½ minutes after each. Friday: 5x200m. on slightly uphill grass surface. Jog 200m. in 90 seconds after each. Walk 5 minutes. 10x100m. in ¾ full effort. Jog 45-60 seconds after each.

SUMMER TRAINING (June and July): On Track, Day 1: 2x(5x400m. in 58-60 seconds each. Jog 400m. in 2½ minutes after each. Jog 5 minutes after first series of 5x400m. before starting second series). Day 2: 2x(5x200m. in 26-27 seconds effort on slightly uphill grass surface. Jog 200m. in 75 seconds after each. Jog 5 minutes after first series of 5x200m.). Day 3: 60 minutes easy walking, jogging and striding in woods (speed play). Day 4: Rest. Day 5: Competition. Day 6: Jog 20 minutes. Then 20m. speed-play including many short sprints. Day 7: 5x300m. in 42-43 seconds each. Jog 90 seconds after each. Then jog 5 minutes. 5x150m. acceleration runs, sprinting final 50m. of each. Jog 150m. after each.

DURATION OF WORKOUTS: 60 minutes, always in the evening. Arne never trains more than once daily. His competitive season extends from May or June to September or October. He rests 3-4 weeks after the competitive season before resuming training again in November each year. He participates in approximately 40 races annually, prefers a fast pace during his races, and often leads. He participates in one or two cross-country races of 3-4 km. per season, and does no indoor running. He does only minimal weight training. Arne has no personal coach, but has received help from several of the Norwegian coaches. He was 1500m. champion of Norway in 1955, 1956, and 1959, and holds the Norwegian record at 1500m. and one mile. Normally he rests one day prior to competition, and eats his final meal 4-5 hours before racing.


## Mehdi Jaouhar

MEHDI JAOUHAR, University of Houston and Moroccan National Team. Age 23, 1971.

BEST MARKS: Marathon, 2:35; 6 miles 29:29.0; 2 miles, 9:10.0; mile, 4:04.2; ¾ mile, 2:53.8; 1000m., 2:28.5, 1000y, 2:09.1. 800m., 1:50.5; 440y, 49.3; 220y, 23.2, 100y, 9.9.

PERSONAL STATISTICS: Born January 1, 1948 at Casablanca, Moracco. 5'8", 132 lbs. Started racing in 1962 at age 14.

PRE-RACE WARM-UP: 3 mile jog; calisthenics; 5x110y at ¾ speed; jog easily until race.

PRE-TRAINING WARM-UP: 3 mile jog and calisthenics; if speed workout, add 4x110y at ¾ speed.

FALL CROSS-COUNTRY TRAINING: Morning runs Monday through Wednesday are 4-6 miles at 7-7:30 per mile. Monday: 10-12 mile run in 1:00-1:15. Tuesday: 4-mile jog, 6x1 mile in 5:00-5:20. Wednesday: Same as Monday. Thursday: 10 mile easy jog. Friday—AM, 4 mile jog. PM 4-6 mile race. Saturday: 10-12 mile run in 1:00-1:15. Sunday: 15-17 mile jog.

WINTER TRAINING: Monday—AM, 4 mile jog. PM, 8-10 mile run. Tuesday—AM, 4 mile jog. PM, 3 mile jog, 25x220y in 32 seconds. Wednesday: 12 mile run. Thursday—AM, 4 mile jog. PM, 8-10 mile run. Friday—AM, Weight training. PM, 10 mile run, hilly course. Saturday: Long period of exercising. Sunday: 15-20 miles.

SPRING/SUMMER TRAINING: Morning workouts Monday through Thursday consist of a 4 mile easy run. Monday: 3 mile jog, 20x220y in 30-32 seconds. Tuesday: 3 mile jog, 8x440y in 65-68 seconds. Wednesday: 3 mile jog, 6x660y in 1:32-1:35. Thursday: 3 mile jog, 5x110y at ¾ speed, 8x220y in 26-27 seconds. Friday: 8-10 mile jog. Saturday—AM, 3 mile jog. PM, Race. Sunday: 15-20 mile run.

A Moroccan title holder at 800m., 1000m., and 1500m., the stocky Jaouhar led off Houston University's 16:27.0 four-mile relay in 1971. As a 15-year-old, he clocked 36.3 for 330y. A fast finisher, he prefers the strategy of follow and kick. He has been coached by Rene Pacheu (1962-63), Jerry MacFadden (64-65), and Van Stichel (Belgium, 65-66). He rests 2 weeks following cross-country and 3 weeks following outdoor track season.

## Michel Jazy

MICHAL JAZY, C.A. Montreuil Club, Paris, France. Age 29, 1965.

BEST MARKS: 5000m., 13:27.6 (6-30-65); 2 miles, 8:22.6 (world record, 6-23-65); 3000m., 7:49.0 (world record, 6-23-65); 2000m., 5:01.6 (world record, 1963); 3000m., 7:49.0 (world record, 6-23-65); 2000m., 5:01.6 (world record, 1963); mile, 3:53.6 (world record, 6-9-65); 1500m., 3:37.8 (1963); 800m., 1:47.1 (1962); 100m., 11.1.

PERSONAL STATISTICS: Born in June, 1936 at Oignies, Northern France. 5'9", 141 lbs. Started racing in 1952 at age 16.

TRAINING: Jazy trained daily, covering 6-15 miles each workout. He often ran cross-country races on Sundays in the winter. He trained two times daily about two or three days a week, covering a total of 22-23 miles on such days. His workouts were not strictly planned. He followed a speed-play (fartlek training philosophy, doing about 80% of his running on paths in the woods and parks which were clearly marked every 100m. In the winter, Jazy ran miles and miles, alternating between easy striding and acceleration runs of 100-300m. to develop aerobic endurance. These winter workouts also included 5-6x400-800m. at 80-85% full effort, each followed by easy walking and jogging. During the spring and summer, special attention was given to training at racing speed or faster. Each week during spring, timed repetitions were run on the track with short recovery periods after each. On the eve of an important race, Jazy usually ran a "rhythm session", at racing speed or slightly faster. For example, prior to the 1965 French National Cross-Country Championship, he ran 3x1000m. in 2:42-2:44. When preparing to run 13:30 for 5000m. he ran 2x500m. in 1:18-1:19; 2-3x1000m. in 2:41-2:42, and again 2x500m. in 1:17-1:18. His training routines can be summarized as follows: (a) Long runs over relatively flat surfaces at varying speeds of 70-75% maximum effort to develop aerobic endurance. (b) Running numerous repetitions of short distances at 95-105% anticipated average racing speed, with short recovery periods after each, to develop anaerobic endurance. (c) Running over

Michel Jazy

uneven surfaces, especially uphill, repeating a series of short distances at 90-100% full effort, to develop speed and local muscular endurance. His heart had exceptional recovery capacity as indicated by this example: During one training session in mid-January, 1965, Jazy ran 8 miles at alternate speeds, followed by 4 times a series of 5x275y in 36-38 seconds, jogging 100-200y after each, with 275y walking-jogging after each set. The 20th and last repetition was run in 30.2. Ten seconds later his heart-rate was 185-190 beats per minute. One minute after completing the 20th repetition of 275y, his heart-rate was 108 beats per minute. In addition to running, Jazy's training involved playing recreational soccer about three times each week.

*Jazy's 1500-meter best came in 1966 with a 3:36.3. He also had a world record 4:56.2 in 1966 in the 2000m. For a number of years he was one of the world's foremost runners 1500m.-5000m. He placed second to Herb Elliott in the 1500m. at Rome and got fourth in the Tokyo Olympic 5000.*

## Stanislav Jungwirth

STANISLAV (STANDA) JUNGWIRTH, Czechoslovakia. Age 27 years, 1957.

BEST MARKS: 800m, 1:47.5; 1500m, 3:38.1; 1 mile, 3:59.1; 3000m, 8:05.4.

PERSONAL STATISTICS: Born August 15, 1930 at Prachatice, Southern Bohemia. Started track competition as a walker in 1946 at age 16.

TRAINING: In order to improve Jungwirth's tempo-endurance, the ability to sustain a fast pace over a relatively long distance, the highest conceivable quantity of repetitions at different speeds were performed. Workouts were done twice daily with the exception of Sundays without regard to the weather and mornings from 6:30 to 8 and afternoons from 4 to 6:30. November thru April: Between 120 and 180 sections of 100m to 800m and tempo control runs up to 200m were run daily, with a light jog between intervals. Throughout this training period the total distance covered progressed from 12 and 15 km to 30 km. The sections were run from month to month with increased tempo by systematic shortening of the interval distances. May thru September: Contained 3 training periods: I. AM workout; PM 4x150m, 7x500m (run 1:12 to 1:09 with the last in 1:05.4), 4x150m. II. AM 5x200m, 10x400m in 58 seconds. III. Training turned from speed to tempo endurance 4x400m and 6x600m (with last 600m in 1:22).

Jungwirth ran the world record time of 3:38.1 for 1500m in 1957 and broke all Czech records from 800-3000m. He was coached by Dr. Ladislav Fischer.

Stanislav Jungwirth

## Kip Keino

KIPCHOGE KIP KEINO, Nairobi, Kenya. Age 32 years. 1972.

BEST MARKS: 100y, 11.0; 220y, 24.0; 440y, 49.0 (t); 880y, 1:46.4; 1500m., 3:34.9; 1 mile, 3:54.4; 3000m., 7:39.6; 2 mile, 8:25.4; 3000m., steeple-chase, 8:23.6; 3 mile, 12:58.6; 5000m., 13:24.2; 6 mile, 27:43; 10,000, 28:06.4.

PERSONAL STATISTICS: Born January 1940 (exact day unknown), at Kapchemoiywo, Nandi District, 5'9", 146 lbs.

WARM-UP: 15 minutes jogging followed by 5 minutes rest.

TRAINING: On his return home from the Tokyo Olympics in 1964, a training schedule was drawn up by Mal Whitfield, former triple Olympic gold medalist and at the time working for the U.S. Information Service in Nairobi. It consisted of: Monday—AM, 3 miles of hill running; Noon, 4x440y in 53-55 seconds; PM, intensive interval work over 330y in 45-46 seconds. Tuesday—AM, 2½ miles roadwork followed by windsprints; PM, 6-8x440y in 53-58 seconds (jog 3 minutes between). Friday—AM, 2½ miles roadwork with heavy boots; Noon, 4½ miles; PM, 1 hour of 175y sprints in 20-25 seconds with 5-6 at full speed. In addition to the basic schedule, according to available time: Once a week 4x¾ mile at 1500m.

pace with 5 minutes jog between each. On days other than the above: 6-8 miles in the morning. Keino worked with this for 2 months before modifying it to meet his own needs. (In March 1966) Monday: 4x440y in 55-58 seconds (jog 440y between). Wednesday: 6-8x440y in 55-58 seconds (jog 440y between). Friday: 4x880y in 1:53-1:56 (jog 5 minutes between). These workouts are concluded with 2x220y, 2x150y and 1x50y. In the morning of each of these days: 6 miles. (In 1970) Thursday, Friday, Saturday and Sunday evenings: repetitions of 200m., 300m., 400m., and/or 600m., (at faster than racing pace). If tired, 3-6 repetitions. If not tired, 12 repetitions. On the mornings of these days: 5-10 miles road run.

Keino does no training during the winter or "wet season." The above workouts eemed fantastically light for modern standards, but it must be kept in mind that a physical training instructor, he is engaged in constant daily activity. Also, ining at high altitude (6000 ft) would seem to offer a "resistance" type of aining.

Keino's achievements are numerous. Among his greatest are the gold medal in the Olympic Games 1500m. in 1968 in the Olympic record of 3:34.9 and the fastest time at high altitude (7,349 ft), and his world record over 3000m. of 7:39.6. He also got the 5000m. silver medal at Mexico City. In Munich, he won the 3000m. steeplechase gold medal with a remarkable 8:23.6, about 11 seconds under his previous best. He placed second to Pekka Vasala in the 1500. He does no weight training. Keino prefers front running so as to maintain control of the race. He has never had a full time coach but has been advised by Mal Whitfield, Mike Wiggs and Bill Dellinger. His training is formulated by himself.

Kip Keino

# Arnd Krüger

ARND KRÜGER, Bayer LeverKusen, West Germany, and UCLA. Age 28, 1972.

BEST MARKS: 3000m., 8:16.2; 2000m., 5:10.0; 1500m., 3:38.8; 1200m., 2:56.0; 1000m., 2:22.6; 800m., 1:47.7; 600m., 1:17.5; 400m., 48.5; 200m., 23.0, 100m., 11.3.

PERSONAL STATISTICS: Born July 1, 1944 at Muhlhausen, Germany. 5'10½". 150 lbs. Started racing in 1958 at age 13.

PRE-RACE WARM-UP: 25 minute jog building up to run, 5 minutes of stretching, 3x100m. strides, 1x200-250m. at race pace, jogging until race time.

PRE-TRAINING WARM-UP: 25 minute jog building up to a run, 5 minutes stretching, 5x100m. strides, 1 lap jog.

FALL CROSS-COUNTRY TRAINING: Monday: 1:45 fartlek alternating minutes per mile pace and 6:30-6:45 pace. Tuesday—AM, 45-60 minutes jog. PM, 1½ hour steady run at 6:30 pace. Wednesday: 2 hour run, pace increasing from 7 minutes to 5:30 per mile. Thursday—AM, 45-60 minutes jog. PM, 1½ hour fartlek as on Monday. Friday—AM, 45-60 minutes jog. PM, 5 mile jog, 20x400m. in 72 seconds with 400m. jog interval, 3 mile jog. Saturday: 2½ hour jog. Sunday: Race or 2 hour buildup as on Wednesday.

WINTER TRAINING: AM, 12½ mile jog to work. PM, 12½ mile run home, pace increasing from 7:00 to 5:30 per mile. Tuesday: Same as Monday. Wednesday: 5 mile jog, 20x400m. in 70-72 seconds with 400m. jog interval, 3 mile jog. Thursday: Same as Monday. Friday: Same as Monday. Saturday: 3 hour jog. Sunday: 1½ hour fartlek with fast runs varying up to 60 seconds per 400m. pace.

SPRING/SUMMER TRAINING: Monday: 2 hour jog. Tuesday—AM, 45 minute jog. PM, 1200m. in 3:00, 10 minute jog, 5x200m., in 26-27 seconds with 200m. jog interval, 10x100m. stride with 100m. jog. Wednesday—AM, 45 minutes jog. PM, 10x400m. in 60 seconds with 400m. jog. Thursday—AM, 45 minute jog. PM, 2x800m. in 2:00, 5x200m. in 26-27 seconds, 10x100m. stride with equal distance jog after each. Friday—AM, 45 minute jog. PM, If race on Sunday, 1½ hour fartlek; if no race, 6x150m. full speed with long recovery. Saturday: If race on Sunday, 45 minute jog, if no race, 2000m., 1600m., 1200m., 800m., 400m. hard pace with equal distance jog after each. Sunday: Race or 1200m. in 2:59, 800m. in 1:56, 400m., in 53 seconds, 10x100m. stride.

In the 800m. Krüger ran 1:50.9 at age 18, 1:48.6 at 19, and 1:47.7 at 22. He was a member of UCLA's world record distance medley team and represented West Germany in the 1500m. at the Mexico City Olympics. He had been coached by Eberhart Mullers, Bert Sumser, Jim Bush, Joe Villarreal, and Heinz

Schlundt. He runs 25-30 races during the outdoor track season which runs from May until late September. He does light weight training in winter.

Kip Keino

# Knut Kvalheim

KNUT KVALHEIM, University of Oregon and Tialve, Oslo, Norway. Age 21 years, 1971.

BEST MARKS: 5000m., 13:55; 3 miles, 13:59; 2 miles, 8:43; 3000m., 8:02.4; 1 mile, 4:00.0; 1500m., 3:46; 1000m., 2:28; 800m., 1:53.3; 400m., .51(e); 200m., 24.5(e); 100m., 12.0 (e); 3000m. Steeplechase, 8:28.4.

PERSONAL STATISTICS: Born June 14, 1950 at Oslo, Norway. 6'3", 168 lbs. Started racing in 1965 at age 14.

PRE-RACE WARM-UP: Begin slow jogging 30:00-40:00 before the race. 10 minutes prior to the race, 2x100y in 14-15 seconds.

PRE-TRAINING WARM-UP: 2-3 miles of slow jogging with last 5-10 minutes at 6:00 mile pace.

FALL CROSS-COUNTRY TRAINING (October-February): Monday—AM (7:30), 3 miles at 6:30-7:00 mile pace. PM (4:00), 4 miles at 6:00-6:30 mile pace. Tuesday—AM, 3 miles at 6:30 mile pace. PM, 5-6x1 mile in 5:00, jog 440y; 3 miles at 6:00-6:30 mile pace. Wednesday—AM, 3 mile at 6:30-6:00 mile pace. PM, 10 mile at 6:00 mile pace. Thursday—AM, 3 miles at 6:30-7:00 mile pace. PM, 18x440y in 68-70 seconds, jog 110y; 3 miles at 6:00-6:30 mile pace. Friday—AM, 3 miles at 6:30-7:00 mile pace. PM, 4 miles at 6:00-6:30 mile pace. Saturday—8-10x880y in 2:15-2:20, jog 220y; 3 miles at 6:00-6:30 mile pace. Sunday—15 mile run, 1st 10 miles at 6:30-7:00 mile pace, last 5 miles at 6:00 mile pace.

WINTER TRAINING (March-April): Monday—AM, 3 miles at 6:30-7:00 mile pace. PM, 4 miles at 6:00-6:30 mile pace; 10-12x110y in 15-16 seconds, rest 10 seconds (Last 2 in 13-14 seconds.) Tuesday—AM, 3 miles at 6:30-7:00 mile pace. PM, 6x1 mile in 5:00, jog 440y; 6x220y in 30-32 seconds; 3 miles at 6:00-6:30 mile pace. Wednesday—AM, 3 miles at 6:30-7:00 mile pace or 30x110y in 16 seconds, rest 10 seconds. PM, 10 miles at 6:00 mile pace; 15x110y in 16-17 seconds. Thursday—AM, 3 miles at 6:30-7:00 mile pace. PM, 30x330y in 50 seconds, jog 110y; 3 miles in 6:30-7:00 mile pace. Friday—AM, 3 miles at 6:30-7:00 mile pace or 30x110y, rest 10 seconds. PM, 4 miles at 6:00-6:30 mile pace. Saturday—10x880y in 2:15, jog 220y; 3 miles at 6:30 mile pace; 15x110y in 15 seconds, rest 10 seconds. Sunday—12-15 miles (10 miles at 6:30-7:00 mile pace, rest at 6:00 mile pace.)

SPRING/SUMMER TRAINING (May-September): Monday and Wednesday— AM, 3 miles at 7:00 mile pace. PM, 6 miles at 6:00 mile pace; 4x110y in 14, 13, 13, & all out. Tuesday—AM, 3 miles at 7:00 mile pace. PM, 1x440y in 59 seconds, jog 330y; 1x660y in 1:30 seconds, jog 330y; 1x440y in 58 seconds, jog 330y; 1x220y in 28 seconds, jog 330y; 6x330y in 42 seconds, jog 330y. Thursday—AM, 3 miles at 7:00 mile pace. PM, 1x880y in 2:00, jog 440y in 56-58 seconds; 2 miles at 7:00 mile pace. Friday—AM, Very light jogging. PM, Very light jogging. Saturday—Race. Sunday—12 mile run.

Does weight training. Coached by Arne Nytro, Bill Bowerman, and Bill Dellinger. Participates annually 30-35 times outdoors and in cross-country 0-10 times per year.

# John Landy

JOHN MICHAEL LANDY, Melbourne University, Australia. Started racing in 1944. Retired in 1956 following Olympic Games at age 26.

PERSONAL STATISTICS: Born April 12, 1930. 5'11", 146 lbs. Performances: Age 14: 100, 11.7; 220 27.8. 15 years: 100, 11.2; 220, 26.2. 16 years: mile, 5:12. 17 years: 880, 2:10; mile, 4:58. 18 years: 440, 54.6, 880, 2:05; mile, 4:41. 19 years: 880, 2:03; mile, 4:38. 20 years: 880, 2:01; mile, 4:19; 100, 10.6; 440, 52.2. 21 years: 880, 1:54.2; 1500m., 3:52.8; mile, 4:11; 3 mile, 14:21; 5000, 14:54. 22 years: 880, 1:53.6; 1500m., 3:44.4; mile, 4:02.1; 2 mile, 8:54.2; 3 mile, 14:00. 23 years: 880, 1:52.9; mile, 4:02; 2 mile, 9:01.6. 24 years: 800m., 1:51.3, 1500m., 3:41.8; mile, 3:58; 2 mile, 8:42.4; 400m., 49.7.

PRE-RACE WARM-UP: 30 minute jogging, striding, short sprints, and calisthenics. "I think a good warm-up, two or three hours before the race, is a sound plan. In hot weather I think you can almost ignore the warm-up in events of one mile and longer."

PRE-TRAINING WARM-UP: No warm-up prior to slow training. Calisthenics and 15 minutes jogging (about 2 miles) prior to fast training. "My ideas on training are orthodox, or at least in line with present trends. Much of the training I did in 1954 was 'against the clock' time trials. This was the only year in which I resorted to that more rigid routine. In all other years my workouts were away from the track itself, and in 1955-56 I did not more than three time trials in training. Such a routine is much less exacting and can be made to fit the particular mood you are in at the time. To my mind the problem of running the mile is simply to blend stamina and speed (such speed as milers have!). Endurance is best obtained through long, slow running and the stopwatch is definitely not necessary except as an occasional check. Speed, on the other hand, is obtained by running at speeds much faster than racing pace, and for distances shorter than 440 yards. Such 'sprints' should be a little below full effort and again a stopwatch is no help in this matter. I feel that running a strict fast-slow quarter mile routine causes you to fall between the two joint aims, producing insufficient pace in each quarter to develop speed and the training is not prolonged or gentle enough to give best results for endurance. With the introduction of workouts over 150, 220, 880 yards, and ¾ mile into the miler's training, Franz Stampfl has achieved fantastic results with his systematic, timed training. But I personally prefer to be guided by intuition (perhaps more accurately, guessing). The system of training must be a matter of personal preference. The controversy is as old as the training schedule of Gunder Hägg and Emil Zatopek. In training I played it very much by ear, and am very much a 'train as you feel' man.''

TRAINING: August, 1952, to November, 1952: Ran to a system of 8 or 12x600 yards, jogging 600 after each. The speed was approximately 65 seconds per 440 pace, and the 600 yard jogs about 4 minutes each. This repetition work was done about 5 times weekly. Ran at least 20 miles a week of long slow running, usually 7 miles being the distance of each run. Best performances *before* this training program were: 880, 1:54.2; 1500m., 3:52.8; mile, 4:10.0; 2 mile, 8:54.2; 3 mile, 14:21.0; 5000m., 14:54.0. And afterwards: 880, 1:53.6; 1500m., 3:44.2; mile, 4:02.1; 2 mile, 9:01.6; 3 mile, 14:00.0. Completed racing 3/18/53, and ran 300 miles, mostly as long runs on the roads. May 25, 27, 30, 1953: 7 miles in 40 minutes, and 30 minutes weight lifting. 5/31/53: 10 miles jogging and striding. 30 minutes weight lifting. 6/1/53: 6x1 mile in 5:00 each. 3 miles in 16 minutes, 30 minutes weight lifting. 6/3/58: 8 miles of 880 yards fast striding, followed by 880 yards jogging. June 8, 10, 12, 14, 17, and 18, 1953: 7 miles in 39 to 40 minutes. 30 minutes weight lifting. June 16, 21, 23, 25, and 27, 1953: 8 miles in 45 minutes. (Running during June and July, 1953, on roads and cross-country. July 13, 15, 16, 18, 19, 1953: 8 miles in 45 minutes. 7/21/53 to 10/1/53: Ran 700x600 yards fast runs at an average of 10x600 each night. Speed was 66 seconds per 440 pace. Jogged 600 after each. October 1, 3, 7, 9, 13, 18, 22, 24, and 30. 1953: 16-19x600. Jog 600 after each. October 2, 4, 6, 8, 12, 16, 21, 23, 25, and 29, 1953: Jog 30 minutes. November, 1953 to December, 1953: Every other day, 20x440 in 62. Jog 440 after each. On alternate days, jog 30 minutes. 12/5/53: mile race in 4:09.8. 12/6/53: 1000m. race in 2:25.5. 12/7/53: 10x440 in 57.5. Jog 440 after each. December 9 & 10, 1953: 6x440 in 62. Jog 440 after. 12/11/53: Rest. 12/12/53: mile race in 58.2, 60.4, 61.6, 61.8 (4:02.0) 1500m. time 3:44.4. December 13, 14, 22, and 26, 1953: Jog 60 minutes. 12/25/53: 4x1 mile in 4:35 each. Jog 440 after each. 12/29/53: 3x¾ mile in 3:05.8, 3:04.2, and 3:02.9. Rest 20 minutes between. 1/2/54: 4x1 mile in 4:20 each. Walk 15 minutes between. 1/4/54: 2 miles training run in 8:53.5. 1/17/54: 4x1 mile barefooted in 4:19.8, 4:18.4, 4:19, and 4:16.7. Walk 15 minutes between. 1/18/54: Jog 30 minutes. 1/20/54: Rest. 1/21/54: Mile race in 4:02.4. February 7 and 20: ¾ mile in 2:57.0 and 2:57.4 respectively. Feb. 2, 17, and 27, 1954: 12x440 in 59-61. Jog 440 after each. 2/19/54: ¾ mile in 3:02.1, 880 in 1:56.1, 440 in 55.9. 2/23/54: Mile race in 4:02.6. 3/2/54: 5x440 in 55.0, 54.6, 54.9, 55.4, and 54.9. Jog 440 after each. March 1, 4, 6, 19, 1954:

12x440 in 59. Jog 440 after each. 4/10/54: 4x¾ mile in 3:06 average. Walk and jog 25 minutes between. 4/26/54 to 5/3/54: Enroute to Turku, Finland. 5/4/54—AM, 4 miles jogging and striding. 4x440 in 61. PM, Jog 2 miles. 8x440 in 59.1 average. (Jog 440 after all 440 repetitions.) 5/5/54—AM, Jog and stride 4 miles. PM, 2 miles in 10:05. 4x440 in 57.8. 5/7/54—AM, Jog 90 minutes. PM, 8x440 in 57.6 average. 5/8/54: Jog 11 laps. Jog and stride alternately for 13 laps, accelerating speed on straight-aways and jogging curves. 5/9/54: Jog 30 minutes. 10x440 in 57.6 average. 5/10/54—AM, 30 minutes jog and stride. PM, 8 laps jog and sprint. 12x100 sprints. Walk 100 yards after each. 5/11/54: Jog 30 minutes. 5/12/54—AM, Jog 3 laps. 8x440 in 58-59. PM, 6x440 in 57.2. 5/13/54: Jog 1½ miles. 10x100m. sprints. Walk 100m. after each. 200m. in 23.3. 5/14/54: 6x300m. in 41.7. Jog 500m. after each. 5x400m. in 57.9. 5/15/54: Jog 3 miles. 6x100m. sprints. Walk 100m. after each. 5/16/54: Jog 10 laps. 10x400m. in 57.6 average. 5/17/54: Jog 15 laps, with 16 acceleration sprints enroute. 300m. in 36.3. 1600m. in 4:20. 5/18/54: Jog 10 laps. 800m. in 1:51.4. Jog 8 laps. 5/20/54: Jog 8 laps. 12x400m. in 58.6. Jog 8 laps. 5/21/54: Jog 8 laps. 2x300 in 35.6 and 36.0. 5/22/54: Jog 3 laps. 11x400m. in 60.4 average. 5/23/54: Jog 20 laps. 440 in 61. 5/24/54: Jog 10 laps. 8x440 in 58.8 average. 5/25/54: Jog 8 laps. 1200m. in 3:00.5. 5/27/54: 17 laps accelerating straightaways, jogging curves. 1600m. steady run. 5 minutes sprinting and jogging. 5/28/54: Jog 10 laps on 300m. track. 2 build-ups per lap. 400m. in 58 seconds. May 29 and 30, 1954: Rest. 5/31/54: Mile race in 56.3, 1:55.7, 2:58, 4:01.6. 6/7/54: Jog 30 minutes. A few sprints. 6/8/54: 30 minute warm-up: Mile race in 59.5, 1:59.5, 3:01.0, 4:01.6. 6/9/54: Jog one hour. 6/10/54: 30 minute jog and stride. A few 300m. runs in 42 seconds. 6/11/54: 1 hour warm-up. 1500m. race in 59.6, 1:59.2, 3:01.4, 3:46.0. June 13 and 14, 1954: Jog and stride one hour. 6/16/54: 300m. in 37 seconds. 400m. in 49.7. 6/19/54: 6 laps warm-up. 1200m. in 2:58.8. 6/21/54: 1 hour warm-up, 3:00 PM to 4:00 PM. Rest until 6:00 PM. Warm-up 6:00 PM to 6:45 PM. WORLD RECORD MILE IN 3:58.0 at Turku, Finland. January 1955 to June, 1955: Walked about 350 miles in 10 mountain hikes. Ran 10-15 miles per week cross country over hilly courses. June, 1955 to October, 1955: 20 minute physical training (calisthenics) daily, including some weight lifting. 50-60 miles per week running, either cross country (6 miles or more per workout) or slow repetitions at 75-85, jogging 50-110 after each. 100-150 miles, hiking. October, 1955, to January, 1956: 20 minutes physical training and weight lifting daily. 50 miles per week fast and slow running. The slow running was cross country or repetitions 75-85, with 110 yards recovery jog after each, on a track with a rise and fall of 30 feet. Up to 15 miles per workout. The fast running was a series of 50-220 yards sprints, never flat out, all run uphill on a grade of 1 in 10. Typical workout was 20x150 yard sprints with 150 yards recovery jog after each. January, 1956, to June, 1956: 20-30 minutes physical training and weight lifting daily. The same sprint work. Cross country runs up to 10 miles each, on easy courses. Repetitions of 440 yards (never timed) at speeds ranging from 60 to 72 seconds.

STRATEGY: "My plan was almost always to run as fast as I could and 'burn off' the opposition during the first three laps of the mile. Since no one seemed anxious to set the pace in my races, I could see no other way of achieving my dual objectives of winning and running the fastest possible time. In my final year, 1956, I modified my 'front running' tactics somewhat. I was determined not to provide a slowing 'target' in the last lap as the Vancouver mile in the 1954 British Empire Games. To achieve this I ran the second lap of the mile faster than the first, but kept the first 880 around 2:01-2:02. Ideally I aimed to run each phase of the race slightly faster than the last, and always leave a good finishing burst for the home stretch. Whereas in 1954 my general plan for a 4 minute mile was 1:58-2:02, in 1956 it was 2:02-1:58. From my first good mile in 1952 to my retirement in 1956, I met 'hot' opposition in the mile on only two or three occasions. Hence my tactical sense was weak. Winning 'from the front' is the most satisfying way and it is always best to lead if there is a reasonable chance of winning. To my mind it is far better to be beaten after setting the pace in 3:58 than to win from behind in 4:10. In big fields of high class runners, such as the Olympic Games, tactics play a great part. A runner in these top races cannot expect to hold an early break throughout the race, and his only chance is to make a bold move within the last 600 yards of the 1500m. and mile events. Most often these races are won in the last 100 yards, and this places great emphasis on the ability to convert from a rapid stride to a finishing sprint. The fast finishers must hang on in the last 440 yards, whereas the 'pace runners' must establish an unbeatable lead shortly before or after the bell. Today, to succeed with an early break before the

John Landy

104

last lap calls for very great strength. The odds will always favor the man behind, who has a physical and psychological advantage, and it will be an exceptional runner, indeed, who wins an Olympic title with front running tactics. Herb Elliott, of course could, and with his clean cut superiority could run the race just about as he liked. But for the man who is only as good as his rivals, to succeed in this way, he must rely heavily on the 'shock' value of his early move, and the failure of the field to pick him up before it is too late. You rarely get two chances in a mile race, and any move should be sudden and decisive. When a runner is passed, he should be 'jumped' as unexpectedly as possible and given no chance to bridge the gap or fight back. Franz Stampfl has likened the effect of the shock this produces to a blow in the stomach, and I can vouch for this in my race against Roger Bannister in 1954. It is particularly hard to make up the leeway in the final straightaway. One should avoid becoming typed as either a 'front runner' or as a 'sitter'. The complete runner should be able to win races both ways. To my mind the only races really worth the 'win at all costs' and 'sitting' policy are National Championships, Olympic Games, etc. On less important races it is much better to take a 'sporting chance' and contribute to the pace setting for a well run and fast mile. If this attitude prevailed in middle distance running, it would not be necessary to introduce rules to outlaw artificial pace making."

# Robin Lingle

RALPH A. LINGLE Jr., University of Missouri. Age 21 years, 1963.

BEST MARKS: Mile (indoors), 4:09.2; 1,000y (indoors), 2:07.6; 880y, 1:50.1; 440y, 49.4.

PERSONAL STATISTICS: Born March 26, 1942 at Philadelphia, Pa. 6'1", 153 lbs. Started racing in 1957 at age 15.

PRE-RACE WARM-UP: 15 minutes jogging, 5 minutes stretching exercises, 10 minutes walking, put on spikes 5 minutes before race and run a couple of straights.

WINTER TRAINING: Monday: 1½ miles continuous running. Tuesday: 6-8x440 varying speeds. Wednesday: 3-4x660 varying speeds. Thursday: Wind sprints. Friday: Light workout if competing; otherwise 8-10x220. Saturday: If not competing, time trial over ¾ mile. Sunday: Rest.

SUMMER TRAINING: Monday: 3-4 miles continuous running. Tuesday: 8-12x440 varying speeds. Wednesday: 3-4x660 varying speeds. Thursday: Wind sprints. Friday: Light workout if competing; otherwise 8-10x220.

Saturday: if not competing, time trial over ¾ mile. Sunday: Rest.

Lingle's training sessions are 45 minutes in duration beginning 3-6 PM. He prefers to rest the day prior to a competition and competes once a week. He does no weight training. He has been coached by Marvin Goldberg, Carleton Crowell, and Tom Botts.

He is a former high school cross country champion. U.S. indoor 1,000y record (2:07.6), 1963. United Kingdom all-comers indoor 1,000y record (2:10.5), 1963.

*In 1964, Robin clocked a 1:49.5 800m. and a 3:42.0 1500. The next year he brought his mile best down to 4:00.3.*

Josef Odlozil

# Josef Odlozil

JOSEF ODLOZIL, Club Sparta, Praha, Czechoslovakia. Age 33 years, 1971.

BEST MARKS: 3000m., 8:10.2; 2000m., 5:01.1; 1 mile, 3:55.6; 1500m., 3:37.6; 1000m., 2:18.6; 800m., 1:48.2; 400m., 49.0; 200m., 22.3; 100m., 10.1 (flying start).

PERSONAL STATISTICS: Born November 11, 1938 at Gottwaldov, Czechoslovakia. 5'9½", 148 lbs. Started racing in 1957 at age 19.

PRE-RACE WARM-UP: 2-3km in 10-15 minutes.

PRE-TRAINING WARM-UP: 2km in 10 minutes.

TRAINING: No fall cross-country training is done. A typical week of *winter training* follows: Monday—AM, Jog 10 minutes. 5x100m. at 17 seconds each. Jog 100m. after each. 4x600m. at 1:50 each. Jog 400m. after each. Rest 3 minutes. 4x600m. at 1:50 each. Jog 400m. after each. 5x100m. at 17 seconds each. Jog 110m. after each. PM, 10km jog. Tuesday—AM, Jog 10 minutes 5x100 at 17 seconds each. Jog 100m. after each. 2 sets of 3x200m.-300m. at 17 sec/100m. Jog 100m. after each. Rest 3 minutes. 2 sets of 3x200m.-500m. at 17 sec/100m. Jog 100m. after each. PM, 5 sets of 5x100m. at 18 seconds each. Jog 100m. after each. Wednesday—AM, 10 minutes jog. 5 sets of 5x100m., 150m., 250m., 350m., at 16 sec./100m. Jog 100m. after each and walk 100m. between sets. PM, Rest. Thursday— AM, 13km jog. PM, weight training. Friday—AM, 10 minutes jog. 5x200m. at 40 seconds each. Jog 100m. after each. 2 sets of 5x600m. at 2 minutes each. Jog 200m. after each. 5x200m. at 40 seconds each. Jog 100m. after each. PM, 10 minutes jog. 10x(100-100-200 at 18 sec/100m. Jog 100m. after each. 10 minutes jog. Saturday—AM, Jog 20 km in 1 hour 40 minutes. PM, Rest. Sunday: Rest.

SPRING/SUMMER TRACK RACING SEASON: Jog 10 minutes before interval training and 5 minutes after. Monday—AM, 12km in 54 minutes. PM, 3 sets of 5x100m. at 15 seconds each. Jog 100m. after each. Tuesday: (All intervals run at 16-16.5 sec./100m. and have a 100m. jog after each.) 5x100m. 200-200-300m. 3 sets of 200-200-400m. 200-200-300m. 5x100m. Wednesday: (All intervals run at 18 sec./100m. and have 100m. jog after each.) 100-100-200m. 200-200-600m. 2 sets of 200-200-800m. 200-200-600m. 100-100-200m. Jog 10 minutes. Thursday: 2 sets of 11x100m. at 16 seconds· each. Jog 100m. after each. Jog 10 minutes. Friday: 5x100m. at 14.5 seconds each. Jog 100m. after each. 5x200m. at 29 seconds each. Jog 100m. after each. Saturday: competition. Sunday: competition.

Usually trains at 9:30 AM spending 90 minutes and in PM spending 60 minutes. Some weight lifting is done with the emphasis on endurance. In addition to holding Czech records in the 1000m, 1500m, and mile, he placed second in the 1964 Tokyo Olympic Games 1500m. and qualified in this event in Mexico in 1968. In 1965 he set a world record in the 2000m. He races from 30 to 35 times a season and rests after this for 3-4 weeks before starting his winter training. Coached by Podebrad Ales.

Tom O'Hara

# Tom O'Hara

THOMAS MARTIN IGNATIUS O'HARA, Loyola University (Chicago). Age 22, 1964.

BEST MARKS: 10,000m., 30:12; 3 miles, 14:30; mile, 3:56.4 (indoors) 1500m., 3:38.1; ¾ mile, 2:59; 1,000 yards, 2:08.6; 880 yards, 1:50.0 (relay); 440 yards, 48.8 (relay); 220 yards, 22.9 (relay); 100 yards, 10.8 (high school time trial).

PERSONAL STATISTICS: Born July 5, 1942 at Chicago, Illinois. 5'9", 130 lbs. Started racing in 1958 at age 16.

PRE-RACE WARM-UP: Start 30 minutes prior to race. Jog 15 minutes. 7-8x100 yards at racing speed. Walk briefly after each. Continue jogging easily until race.

PRE-TRAINING WARM-UP: Jog 3 miles at speed of 7-8 minutes per mile. Warm-down with 2-3 miles at same speed after training.

SUMMER TRAINING (August, 1963): Run alternately 17 miles easily one day and 10 minutes at a faster speed the following day, seven days per week.

FALL TRAINING (September 1 to December 1, 1963): Sunday: Run 17 to 20 miles continuously at an easy speed. No warm-up or warm-down. Monday and Saturday: 20x440 yards in 75 seconds each. Walk 30 seconds between. Tuesday: 10 miles continuous running, faster than Sunday. Wednesday: 16x440 yards in 72 seconds each. Jog 440 yards in 2½ minutes between. Thursday: 10-12 miles fartlek. Friday: 440-880- ¾ mile, 880-440 at speed of 77 seconds per 440 yards. Jog an equal distance after each.

WINTER TRAINING (December, 1963 through March, 1964): Sunday: 17-20 miles easy run outdoors. Monday: 12-16x440 yards in 63-64 seconds each. Jog 220 yards in 90 seconds after each. Indoors. Tuesday: 24x220 yards in 32 seconds each. Jog 220 yards in 90 seconds after each. Indoors. Wednesday: 10-12 miles continuous run outdoors, or 5x660 yards in 1:36, jog 440 yards in 1½ minutes between. Indoors. Thursday: Rest in case of competition Friday. Otherwise, 16x220 yards in 30.5. Jog 220 yards in 90 seconds between. Friday: Race. Otherwise, 660 yards in 1:32. Jog 10 minutes. Then 5-6x330 yards in 43 seconds. Jog 220 yards between. If racing on Saturday, then rest Friday. Saturday: Race. Otherwise, 20x440 yards in 75 seconds each. Walk 30 seconds between.

SPRING TRAINING (April to July, 1963): Sunday: 10 miles continuous run. Monday: 12x440 yards in 62 seconds each. Jog 220 yards between. Tuesday and Thursday: 880 yards in 2:04. Jog 880 yards. Then 10x220 yards in 29 seconds each. Jog 220 yards between. Jog 880 yards. Then 660 yards in 1:28. Wednesday: 2x¾ mile in 3:08 each. Jog 10 minutes between.

Friday: In case of competition on Saturday, rest on Friday evening and run only 15x110 yards fast striding on Friday morning. In the absence of a race on Saturday, repeat Monday's training. Saturday: Competition. Otherwise, 24x220 yards in 32 seconds each. Jog 220 yards between.

MORNING WORKOUTS: During fall, winter, and spring he trains 30-50 minutes between 8:00 and 9:00 AM, Monday through Friday, five days per week. Two of these morning workouts are devoted to short sprints and jogging. Three of these workouts consist of 3-4 miles of easy, continuous running.

O'Hara's evening workouts took 90-120 minutes, starting at 3:00 PM. He ate four hours before racing. He ran five cross-country races, about ten indoor races, and ten outdoor races per year. He was coached by Jerry Weilland at Loyola. Prior to entering Loyola and during summer months while on vacation from university, he sought the advice of renowned Chicago high school and DePaul University coach, Don Amidee. He did no weight training. If his racing objective was merely to win, he preferred following to pace-setting. If his objective was achieving a fast time, he was not opposed to leading if the pace of his opponents proved to be too slow.

O'Hara was one of history's finest indoor milers and set a world record of 3:56.4 in 1964.

## Hector Ortiz

HECTOR LOUIS ORTIZ, Western Kentucky University, Bowling Green, Kentucky. Age 20 years, 1969.

BEST MARKS: 6 miles, 30:20.4; 3 miles, 14:17; 2 miles, 9:10; 1 mile, 4:08.1; 880y, 1:55.3; 440y, 50.9; 220y, 24.0(t); 100y, 10.7(t).

PERSONAL STATISTICS: Born May 25, 1949. 5'8", 138 lbs. Started racing in 1963 at age 14.

PRE-RACE WARM-UP: Jogging-light exercise-jogging-fast striding which takes 60 minutes. Total distance jogged is 2-3 miles.

PRE-TRAINING WARM-UP: Jogging-stretching-jogging which takes 10-20 minutes. Total distance jogged is 1-2 miles.

FALL CROSS-COUNTRY TRAINING: Monday—AM (6:30), 5 mile easy run on grass. PM (3:30), One hour run on grass at under 6 minutes per mile. Tuesday—AM (6:30), 5 mile easy run on grass. PM, (3:30), 24x440 in 75. Jog 220's. Wednesday—AM (6:30), 30 minutes of 100y hill sprints, with

220 recovery jog. PM (3:30), 10 mile run on rolling Golf Course in under 60 minutes. Thursday—AM (6:30), One hour run at easy pace. PM (3:30), 3x(20x220 in 35. Jog 220's. Walk 10 minutes between sets.) 10x110 at fast stride. Jog to where preceding run finished and start. Friday—AM (6:30). One hour easy run on grass—cover around 6 miles. PM (3:30), 2x(20x110. Odd 110's easy, and even 110's hard. Walk 55. Walk 880. 10x220 in 35. Jog 110's. Walk 880. 5x440 in 70. Jog 220's.) Saturday— AM (6:30), 30 minute jog on grass. PM, Race. Sunday—1½ hour easy run on grass.

WINTER TRAINING: (AM workouts dropped in winter). Monday: 4x(10x110). Odd 110's hard and even 110's easy. Walk 55). Tuesday: One hour road run. "Just cover what I feel like." Wednesday: 2x(10x220) in 33. Jog 220's. 7-10 minutes between sets. Thursday: 1½ hour run on golf course. Friday: One hour run on grass. 8-12x440 in 68-72. Jog 220's. Not timed by the coach. Saturday: Two hour run on grass at 6 to 7½ minutes per mile. Sunday: 45 minute run hard. Under 6 minutes per mile.

SPRING/SUMMER TRAINING: Monday—AM. One hour run on grass at 6½ to 7 minutes per mile. PM, 15x110 in 15. Walk 55. Walk 440. 5x440 in 63-65. Start each run when pulse returns to 120. Walk 880. 20x220 in 33. Jog 220's. 5x440 in 63-65. Recovery—120 pulse. 20x110. Odd runs in 17 and even runs in 15. Walk 55. Jog 2 miles. Tuesday—AM. One hour jog on grass. PM. 12x220 in 33-32-31-33-32 etc. Jog 220's. Walk 880. 3x330 in 45. Jog 110's. Walk 1320y. 2x440 in 60 or under. Recovery—120 pulse.

Hector Ortiz

20x220 in 33. Jog 220's. Jog 2 miles. Wednesday—PM, 15x110. The first in 18-19 and the rest in 13-15. Walk 55. 12x440 at race pace. Jog 220's. 10x110y in 13-14. Walk back to where preceding run finished and start. Jog 2 miles. Thursday—PM, 3x880 in 2:00 or under. Interval of 5-7 minutes. Rest 30 minutes. 2x440 in under 60. Recovery—120 pulse. Friday—PM, 10x110 at race pace. 4-6x440 at race pace. 20-40 at "the way I feel." Walk 55. Saturday: Race. Sunday: One hour run on grass at 6:30-6:45 per mile.

Ortiz weight-trains 2-3 times weekly during the winter and the late summer. Included in his routine is sets of 10 squat jumps with 10 lbs. for his legs. Coached by Dick Simmons and Burch Oglesby. Runs 10 cross-country, 3-4 indoor, and 15 outdoor races annually. Trains 1 hour in the morning and 1½-2 hours in the evening. He has a great finish. When he ran 4:10.1 for a New York State H.S. record in 1968 he had a 58.0 last 440. All his track workouts are run on an all-weather surface.

*Hector Ortiz recorded a 4:00.4 in 1970.*

## Ken Popejoy

KENNETH LEE POPEJOY, Michigan State University and Glen Ellyn (Illinois) Road Runners. Age 22 years, 1972.

BEST MARKS: 6 miles, 28:55; 2 miles, 9:04 (indoors); 1 mile, 3:59.7; 1500m., 3:41.9; ¾ mile, 2:56.1 (t); 1000y, 2:11.0; 880y, 1:48.3; 660y, 1:20.9 (in 880y); 440y, 48.5; 330y, 34.9 (t); 220y, 22.9 (in 330y), 110y, 10.5.

PERSONAL STATISTICS: Born December 9, 1950 at Glen Ellyn, Illinois. 5'8", 115-120 lbs. Started racing in 1964 at age 13.

PRE-RACE WARM-UP: (1 hour before race) Jog 1 mile and sprint hard 220y-330y. Rest until ½ hour before race. Jog 1 mile, 5-10 minutes of calisthenics, 4-5x110y-150y buildups. Relax 5 minutes prior to race.

PRE-WORKOUT WARM-UP: Jog 2½-3 miles, 10-15 minutes of calisthenics, 1-2x110y buildups.

FALL CROSS-COUNTRY TRAINING: In addition to the following afternoon (3 PM) workouts, on weekdays Popejoy does a morning (6:30 AM) workout of an easy 3 (end of weekdays)-6 miles (beginning of weekdays). The weekday PM workouts are performed on a golf course and involve a 3½ mile jog to and 2½-3 mile return. Monday: 1x3 mile, 1x2 mile, 1x1 mile (stand 5 minutes between), 4x300y sprints (300y jog between). Tuesday:

10x880y (stand 2 minutes between). Wednesday: 6x1 mile (stand 4 minutes between), 3x330y buildups (300y jog between). Thursday: 1x2 mile, 30 minute fartlek. Friday: Jog 6 miles. Saturday: competition. Sunday: 12 miles easy.

WINTER TRAINING: On weekdays Popejoy does a morning workout of 3-4 miles. Monday: 1x¾, 1x880y, 1x660y, 1x440y (walk and jog 2-5 minutes between depending on distance). Tuesday: 11x440y (440y walk between). Wednesday: 1x¾ mile, 10 seconds rest, 1x440y. Thursday: 2x880y-440y-220y (440y jog between). Friday: Jog 5 miles. Saturday: competition. Sunday: 10 mile run (last 4 miles @ 5:45 pace).

SPRING/SUMMER TRAINING: On weekdays Popejoy does a morning workout of 3½-5 miles. Monday: 1x¾ mile, 880y-660y-440y-330y-220y-110y (between jog distance of next interval). Tuesday: 6x440y-220y (jog 440y between). Wednesday: 1x660y, 1x500y, 1x440y (jog 440y between). Thursday: 3x440y (walk 440y between). Friday: 3x110y @ 14-15. Saturday: competition. Sunday: 8-10 mile run (last 4-5 miles @ 5:30-6:00 pace).

Weight training, performed by Popejoy 2-3 times per week, consists of 3 sets of 10 reps of bench press (working up to 110 lbs.), curls (60 lbs.), and military press (90 lbs.). Popejoy likes to get a good start and run near the front, eventually utilizing a good kick at the end of the race. He has been coached by Jim Arnold/Dave Shinneman (high school) and Jim Gibbard (college).

## Duwayne Ray

DUWAYNE W. RAY, Chico State College, Chico, California. Age 23 years, 1969.

BEST MARKS: 3 miles, 14:27; 2 miles, 9:04; mile, 4:02.9; 880 yards, 1:50.5; 660 yards, 1:23; 440 yards, 48.3.

PERSONAL STATISTICS: Born March 31, 1946 at Vian, Okla. 5'10", 148 lbs. Began racing in 1962 at age 16.

PRE-RACE WARM-UP: Two mile jog with pickup on last 880; 100-yard sprints with 3-4 hard immediately before race; stretching. 3-5 miles in 25-45 minutes.

PRE-TRAINING WARM-UP: 3-6 miles and sprints in 20-45 minutes.

FALL CROSS-COUNTRY TRAINING: Monday—AM, 3-5 miles with 12x220 or

113

16x110 afterwards on track. PM, 10-14 miles at easy pace (10-14 mph). Tuesday—AM, same. PM, 10 mile run; 330s, 220s, 110s each x 10 with 110 jog interval and 440 between sets. Wednesday—AM, same. PM, 8-10 miles at 8-9 mph; 8-10x110. Thursday—AM, same. PM, 8-14 miles at 8-9 mph; 8-10x220 at 27-29 seconds. Friday—PM, easy jog 2-4 miles. Saturday—PM, Competition. Sunday: 12-17 hard miles in mountains.

WINTER TRAINING: Basically same as fall cross country training.

SPRING/SUMMER TRACK TRAINING: Monday—AM, 3-5 miles with 12x220 or 16x110 afterwards on track. PM, 10-12 miles at 8-9 mph; 12x110 at 9/10 speed. Tuesday—AM, same. PM, 25-45 minute run; 6x330-220-110 with 110 jog interval and 220 standing between sets. Pace of 41-28-12. Wednesday—AM, same. PM, 25-45 min run; 8x220 at 38-39 with 220 jog interval. Thursday—AM, same. PM, 25-45 minute run; 8x220 at 27-29 with 110 jog interval. Friday—PM, easy jog 2-4 miles. Saturday: Competition. Sunday: 10 miles at 8-9 mph; 4x440 on track.

Coached by Larry Burleson, Bob Hoegh, Leonard Kaiser. Runs 10 times in cross country, twice indoors and 16 times outdoors. No weight training. 1968 California JC state mile champ at Modesto JC.

DuWayne Ray

## Alan Robinson

ALAN VICTOR ROBINSON, Southern Illinois University. Age 21 years, 1969.

BEST MARKS: 5000m., 13:59.6; 2 miles, 8:49.0; mile, 4:01.5; 1500m., 3:41.3; 1000m., 2:27.0; 800m., 1:51.5; 400m., 52.6; 100y, 11.5(e).

PERSONAL STATISTICS: Born May 16, 1948 at Sydney, Australia. 6', 145 lbs. Started racing in 1963 at age 15.

PRE-RACE WARM-UP: This follows no set pattern but includes 1-3 miles of jogging plus light stretching exercises.

PRE-TRAINING WARM-UP: "I'm usually impatient and hate to fool around warming up, otherwise I lose interest and concentration and have a lousy session."

FALL TRAINING (Australia, 1968): On weekdays Robinson did 1 or 2 workouts per day, usually 5 miles per session. This was done either at even pace or as fartlek with fast bursts of 1/5 to 1½ mile. Terrain included hilly bush tracks, beaches, golf courses, or roads. Sunday morning workout was usually 10-15 miles hard over hills followed by 6 miles of fartlek in the afternoon.

Alan Robinson

WINTER TRAINING (Southern Illinois, 1969): Morning workout Monday through Thursday consisted of a ¾ mile jog gradually increasing to near 5:00 per mile pace for 4 miles followed by a mile jog. Afternoon workouts Monday through Thursday: 15x330y in 46-50 seconds with 60-90 second jog interval, or 20x440y in 70 seconds with 220y jog, or 10-15x220y, each done outdoors on dirt-grass straightaway. Friday: 5 mile easy jog. Saturday: Race, mile-2-mile double. Sunday: 12 mile run on roads with pace just above 5 minutes per mile.

SPRING TRAINING: Much the same as winter workouts except that speed work was done on cinder track. Typical workouts: 20x440y in 65-70 seconds with 220y jog interval, or 10x220y in 27 seconds with 220y jog, or 20x220y in 29 seconds with 220y jog, or 10-15x330y in 45 seconds.

Robinson in a February 1969 indoor meet tripled in the mile. 880y and 2 mile with times of 4:03.5, 1:53.1, and 8:59.0, all within a 1½-hour period. He has been coached by Jack Gibson (1964-65) and Lewis Hartzog (1969). "I like to talk to coaches, but have learned most from fellows like Laurie Toogood, John Farrington, and lately Oscar Moore."

He trains 52 weeks per year. His weight training consists of presses, curls, cleans, squats, and rowing.


## Istvan Rozsavolgyi

ISTVAN ROZSAVOLGYI, Honev Club, Budapest, Hungary. Age 32 years, 1961.

BEST MARKS: 10,000m., 31:05; 5000m., 13:59.8; 3000m., 7:53.6; 2000m., 5:02.2 (world record); 1500m., 3:38.9; 1000m., 2:19; 800m., 1:48.4; 400m., 51.5; 300m., 37.0; 200m, 24.5; 100m., 12.0 seconds.

PERSONAL STATISTICS: Born in 1929 at Budapest, Hungary. 5'9", 126 lbs. Started racing in 1952 at age 23.

PRE-RACE WARM-UP: Jog 4000m., 5-10 minutes calisthenics. 4-6x60-80m., fast runs, each progressively faster. Walk or jog briefly after each.

PRE-TRAINING WARM-UP: Same as pre-race warm-up, except only 3000m. jogging.

WINTER TRAINING (evening workouts): Day 1: 20x100m. Day 2: 15x100m. 2x(10x200m.). 20x100m. Day 3: 15x100m. 10x400m. 2x(10x100m.) Day 4: 15x100m. 3x(10x100m.). Day 5: 60 minutes running at a speed strictly according to personal inclination. Day 6: 15x100m., 15x600m. easy. 10x100m. Day 7: 2 hours cross-country running and walking at speeds according to personal inclination.

SUMMER TRAINING (evening workouts): Day 1: 1 hour easy running and walking. Day 2: 10x100m. 5x200m. 3x400m. 10x100m. Days 3 and 6: 20x100m. Day 4: 15x100m. 3x600m. fast. 10x100m. Day 5: 10x100m. Day 7: competition.

These workouts are seldom timed, and are preferably run on a marked grass area. The speed of these repetitions varied from racing speed to full sprint speed, and is often varied within the same set. For example, in a set of 20x100m. repetitions, every second, third, or fourth 100m. might be full speed, and the remaining 100m. repetitions might be racing speed. His 400 and 600m. repetitions are seldom faster than racing speed. For recovery between repetitions, Rozsavolgyi usually jogs for a distance equal to the length of the preceding fast repetition. For recovery between sets of repetitions, he walks or jogs in accordance with the severity of the preceding set. For example, in the 3x(10x100m.) phase of a workout, he might run every third 100m at full speed, and the remaining 100m. repetitions at racing speed. He would jog 100m. in about 30 seconds after each 100m. repetition. After each set of 10x100m., he might walk and jog easily for 3-5 minutes.

Istvan Rozsavolgyi               Dan Waern

The speed of Rozsavolgyi's summer training is somewhat faster than in winter. He runs 4000-7000m. easily each morning at 7:00 AM, and takes the above described workouts at 4:00 PM daily. These take up to 40 minutes in the morning, and 2 hours of evenings. He does not rest prior to competition, but decreases the volume of running prior to racing as noted above. His last meal is eaten 4 hours prior to competition. He participates in 4 cross-country, 3-6 indoor, and approximately 20 outdoor races annually. Rozsavolgyi's outdoor track racing season starts in May and ends in October, after which he rests one month prior to starting winter training. He uses no fixed racing tactics, is quite capable of leading from gun to finish, but is noted for his fast finishing kick. He uses weight training only formally, lifting 30-50 kg. in lifts designed to strengthen the legs. However, he places little emphasis on weight training.

Rozsavolgyi was coached from 1952 to 1956 by Mihaly Igloi, and from 1957 through 1961 by Gyula Aufol. He won the bronze medal in Rome in 1960. In answering the questionnaire which described his training, Rozsavolgyi pointed out that the above training is typical of that used by Igloi in training other renowned athletes in Hungary. Rozsavolgyi announced his retirement at the conclusion of the 1961 season.


## Peter Stewart

PETER JOHN STEWART, Birchfield Harriers and Aberdeen Athletic Club, Scotland. Age 24 years, 1971.

BEST MARKS: 5000m., 14:03.6; 2 miles, 8:26.8; 3000m., 7:55.2; 3000m. SC, 9:33.0; mile, 3:57.4; 1500m, 3:39.0; 800m., 1:50.9.

PERSONAL STATISTICS: Born August 8, 1947 at Musselburgh, Scotland. 5'7", 133 lbs. Started racing in 1962 at age 14.

WARM-UP: 1-1½ mile jog; 10 minute calisthenics; 4x100y strides if track session to be done.

WINTER TRAINING: Monday: 5 miles. Tuesday: 10 miles. Wednesday: 5 miles. Thursday: 10 miles. Friday: 5 miles. Saturday: 10 miles. Sunday: 10 miles.

SUMMER TRAINING: Monday: 5 miles. Tuesday: 10x440y in 61 seconds. Wednesday: 5 miles. Thursday: 6x880y in 2:10. Friday: Rest. Saturday: Race. Sunday: 10 miles easy fartlek.

Stewart is holder of the United Kingdom records in the 2 mile and 1500m. He does two workouts daily year around. Three times per week he does weight training after running. His workouts last 30 minutes in morning and 1½ hour in evening. He is coached by Geoff Warr.

*In 1972, Stewart recorded an excellent 3:55.3 mile. An injury prevented him from competing in the Olympic Games. He is the brother of Ian Stewart, 1970 Commonwealth Games 5000m. champion and Munich bronze medalist.*

## Terry Sullivan

TERRANCE A. SULLIVAN, Federation of Rhodesia and Nyasaland, Central Africa. Age 25, 1960.

BEST MARKS: 2 miles, 9:08.5; mile, 3:59.8, 1500m., 3:42.8; ¾ mile, 3:00.0; 880 yards, 1:49.8; 660 yards, 1:20.0; 440 yards, 49.4; 330 yards, 34.0; 220 yards, 22.8; 100 yards, 10.6 seconds.

PERSONAL STATISTICS: Born September 7, 1935 at Johannesburg, South Africa. 6'2", 146 lbs. Started racing in 1949 at age 14.

PRE-RACE WARM-UP: Requires about 40 minutes. Slow jog for 1½ miles. 4-6x60 yards at slightly faster than racing pace. Walk briefly after each. Rest until race.

PRE-TRAINING WARM-UP: 2-3 miles slow jog. 10 minutes stretching exercises.

WINTER TRAINING: (September, 1960 to January, 1961) Day (1): 30 minutes continuous run near top speed covering 5-6 miles, under trees in park or on open fields. Day (2): 20x200 yards sprints. Walk 60 seconds after each. Day (3): Grass track. 8x330 yards in 40 seconds each. Walk 5 minutes after each. Day (4): Weight training only. Standing barbell press, alternate barbell press, bench press, upright rowing, barbell curl, and push-ups. Day (5): Fartlek (speed-play) in woods or fields for 1 hour, or 3x¾ miles in woods as fast as possible, walking 10 minutes after each. Day (6): 10 miles run over country as fast as possible. Day (7): Rest.

MID-COMPETITIVE SEASON TRAINING: (April, 1960) Monday: 4x880 yards in 2:00-2:03 each. Walk 10-15 minutes after each. Tuesday: 8x330 yards in 38-39. Walk 5 minutes between. Wednesday: 3x¾ mile in 3:07. Walk 15 minutes between. Thursday: 5 miles slow jogging. Friday: Rest. Saturday: Competition. Sunday: 7-10 miles in woods at near full speed, starting at 10:00 AM, followed by swimming. each of the above workouts is followed by 10 minutes walking as a warm-down. He never trains more than once daily. Duration of workouts—90 minutes, starting at 4:30 PM. His competitive track season starts in January and ends in July. He rests 6 weeks following track season prior to starting winter training in preparation for the next season. Sullivan participates in approximately 25 track races annually. He last eats 3½ hours prior to competition, is self-coached, and has no serious rival at middle-distance running in his native land. He has been 880 yards and mile champion of his country for the past six years, and participated in the 1500m. in the 1960 Olympic Games at Rome.

Sullivan uses no fixed racing tactics, and is prepared to lead or follow as racing circumstances demand. However, in fast mile competition he prefers to be in 3rd or 4th position with 660 yards to go, and finish with a sustained kick over the entire final 440 yards.

# Fanie Van Zÿl

STEPHANES JOHANNES VAN ZÿL, Potchefstroom University, South Africa. Age 21 years, 1969.

BEST MARKS: 5000m, 14:03.0; 2-miles, 8:50.0; mile, 3:59.3; 1500m, 3:41.1; 1000m, 2:21.1; 800m, 1:45.6; 400m, 47.6; 200m, 22.0; 100m, 10.6 (e).

PERSONAL STATISTICS: Born July 7, 1948 at Randfontein, South Africa. 5'10", 140 lbs. Started racing in 1965 at age 15.

PRE-RACE WARM-UP: Alternately jog and walk 100m 6-8 times; run 800m slowly; 10-minutes of calisthenics; 2x150y at ¾ pace; 1-2x150y after putting on spikes.

PRE-TRAINING WARM-UP: 1½-mile jog, 10-minutes of calisthenics, ½-mile jog.

FALL CROSS-COUNTRY TRAINING: Morning workouts Monday through Friday are steady runs of 30-40 minutes through farm country. Monday: 1-hour cross-country run at medium pace, about 10 miles. Tuesday: 1-hour fartlek. Wednesday: 1-hour run (8-10 miles) over hilly terrain. Thursday: Same as Tuesday. Friday: Morning workout only with 6-minutes of calisthenics midway in the run and following the run. Saturday: 7-mile race. Sunday: 1½-2-hour relaxed run (16-20 miles).

WINTER TRAINING: This is the same as his fall training, since the cross-country season extends from April to September.

SPRING/SUMMER TRAINING: Monday—AM, 20-30 minute run (4-5 miles). PM, 10x400m in 58 seconds with 400m jog after each. Tuesday—AM, 20-30 minute run. PM, 50-minute run through the country. Wednesday— 1x400m, 4x200m, 8x100m with equal distance jog after each. Thursday— 50-minute easy run. Friday—20-30-minute jog, 5-10-minutes of calisthenics. Saturday—Race. Sunday—1-hour jog in the country.

"I do hill training in early stages of track racing season, running up and down the same hill, which is approximately ½-¾ mile long, about 5 times." Van Zÿl runs about 40 races during the track season, which extends from October to April in South Africa. His 1:45.6 800m. in 1970 broke the S.A. national record. He is noted as a top competitor with a swift finishing kick. He is coached by Jan Barnard.

*Van Zÿl brought his best 800m. down to 1:45.6 in 1970, ranking 7th internationally. He also had a 3:59.0 mile that year. Injured in 1971, he really came into his own in 1972 with a highly successful U.S. tour, capped by a 3:37.9 1500 and a 3:56.0 mile. He ranked fifth world-wide in the 1500/Mile.*

## Dan Waern

DAN JOHN RUNE WAERN, Orgryte Idrottssallskap, Gothenburg, Sweden. Age 27, 1960.

BEST MARKS: 3000m., 7:59.6; 2000m., 5:05.6; mile, 3:58.5; 1500m., 3:38.6; 1000m., 2:17.8 (world record); 800 yards, 1:48.8; 800m. 1:47.8.

PERSONAL STATISTICS: Born January 17, 1933 at Skoeldinge, Sweden. 6', 150 lbs. Started racing in 1948 at age 15.

PRE-RACE WARM-UP: Slow jogging 40 minutes. 12-15x80-100 yards fast runs, mixed with jogging, during last 20 minutes. No calisthenics.

PRE-TRAINING WARM-UP: 15 minutes slow jogging. No fast runs. Waern uses the first runs of his workout as the last part of the warm-up.

WINTER TRAINING: Monday and Thursday: 15x400m. in 67 seconds. Jog 1½-2 minutes between. Tuesday and Friday: 6x800m. in 2:25-2:30. Jog 2½-3 minutes after each. Wednesday and Saturday: 45 minutes easy speed-play. Sunday: 6 miles fast speed-play, with 6-7 uphill sprints. Influenced by Herb Elliott, Waern ran during the winter of 1958-59 from 10 to 12 uphill sprints of 70-80 yards each prior to the above interval training. Since the indoor track at the Ullevi Stadium in Gothenburg has been available during 1959-60 for training, Waern does his interval training there and the uphill running is limited to the Sunday training. He does not engage in weight training.

SUMMER TRAINING: Monday and Thursday: 8-10x400m. in 54-58 seconds. Jog 5-6 minutes after each. Tuesday and Friday: 5x800m. in 1:58-2:02. Jog 8-10 minutes after each. Wednesday: 25x200m. or 270m. on grass, not timed. Jog 200m. after each. The pace for 270m. (300 yards) is 42-43 seconds. Saturday: 30 minutes speed-play. Sunday: Race. Following the race, 10x80-100 yards at full speed.

STRATEGY: During the first lap, Waern attempts to be in second place. With one or two laps remaining before the finish, depending upon the character of the race, he makes a hard kick and attempts to leave his opposition behind with a terrific pace. He always runs for fast times.

Waern is self-coached, but has received advice from Erik Nilsson of Gaffle, Gosta Olander of Valadalen, and Gunnar Carlsson, the National Coach of Sweden. Before major competition, Waern likes to go to Valadalen resort hotel for a week or more, where he trains twice daily and relaxes with fishing and hill-climbing under the care of Gosta Olander. After such a session with Olander he is filled with enthusiasm and ready for his best performance.

Always a dangerous competitor, his fierce finishing wallop gave him fourth place in the 1500m. final at the 17th Olympiad in Rome.

## John Whetton

JOHN WHETTON, Sutton-in-Ashfield AC, England. Age 27 years, 1969.

BEST MARKS: 3 miles, 13:44.8; 2 miles, 8:43.6; mile, 3:57.7; 1500m., 3:39.9; 880, 1:50.4; 440, 50.8.

PERSONAL STATISTICS: Born September 6, 1941 at Mansfield (Notts) England. 5'10", 148 lbs.

PRE-RACE WARM-UP: 1¼ miles easy jog; stretching mobility exercises; 6 "strides" of increasing stride length and speed followed by 10 minutes recovery prior to competition.

WINTER TRAINING: Monday—AM, 50 minutes fartlek on hills. PM, 30 minutes continuous run on grass. Tuesday: 10-12 mile run in the country. Wednesday—AM, 4-5 mile fast run in country. PM, 30 minutes run on grass. Thursday: 50 minutes fartlek on hills. Friday: Rest. Saturday: Cross-country race or 50 minutes hard run in woods and hills. Sunday: 45 minute competitive "power-speed" run in Charnwood Forest, Loughborough.

SUMMER TRAINING: Monday—AM, 50 minutes fartlek in hills. PM, 30 minutes continuous run on grass. Tuesday—AM, 3x(5x330 in 42-43 seconds with 110 jog between each) and 5 minutes between sets. PM, 30 minutes run on grass. Wednesday: 5 timed runs at race pace: 1:50, 1:50,

3:45, 1:50, 1:50, all within 1 hour, on graas. Thursday: 50 minutes fartlek on hills. Friday: Rest. Saturday: Competition or 10-12 mile run in woods. Sunday: Competitive track work of 10x330 in 41 seconds with 2 minute recovery or 3x¾ mile in 3:02 with 10 minutes rest.

Whetton was a 1500m. finalist at both the 1964 and 1968 Olympic games, placing fifth in '68, and ranking 5th in the world the latter year. A physical education lecturer by profession, he trains six days per week, often twice per day, 45-60 minutes per session. He believes in hard training the day after a race, but not on the track. Prior to the 1968 Olympics he did 50x100y very fast with 30 seconds maximum rest, several times per week. He trains with weights twice weekly from September to April only. He has been coached by Bill Coyne, Geoff Gowan, and Robbie Brightwell.

Regarding his fartlek training he states, "When I come to a hill, I run up it *flat out.* I do this all year 'round. I am never short of speed."

*In 1969, Whetton won the European Championships 1500 in a lifetime best of 3:39.4. He ranked 6th in the world that year. His best mile of 3:57.7 was recorded in 1970.*

John Whetton

## Sydney Wooderson

SYDNEY CHARLES WOODERSON, Blackheath Harriers.

BEST MARKS: 5000m., 14:08.6; 3 miles, 13:53.2; 2 miles, 9:05; mile, 4:04.2; 1500m., 3:48.4; ¾ mile, 2:59.5 WR; 880, 1:49.2 WR; 800m., 1:48.4 WR; 440, 49.2.

PERSONAL STATISTICS: Born August 30, 1914. 5'6", 125 lbs. Started racing in 1926 at age 12 and quit in 1948 at age 34.

PRE-RACE WARM-UP: Mile jog with 150 yard bursts en route.

PRE-TRAINING WARM-UP: 2 miles easy jog.

WINTER TRAINING: Easy striding 2-4 miles 5 times a week.

SUMMER TRAINING: Monday: Fast sprints for 2 miles. Tuesday: 2x660 fast. Wednesday: 1¼ mile fast, mile jog with 150 yard bursts en route. Thursday: ¾ mile fast. Friday: Rest or easy 2 miles. Saturday: Race.

Time of workouts: 7 PM for about 2 hours.

Ran 4:29.8 as a high school miler in 1933 and set world records for 800m., 880, and mile (4:06.4) in 1938. Wooderson was the European Champion at 1500m. in 1946. In 1939 he became the first man to break 3 minutes for ¾ mile. He developed rheumatism in the summer of 1944 and spent 4 months in the hospital where he was told he would never race again. However, 6 months later he was racing. In the 1945 season he recorded British records for 1500m. and mile. In 1946 he set British records for 3 miles, 5000m., and a personal 2 mile best. His last race was in 1948 where he captured the 9 mile English cross-country championship. At the end of his career he held 7 British records from 800m.-5000m. and was undefeated in dual international meets. His chance at an Olympic medal was denied him in 1936 by a cracked ankle bone and later by the war. He preferred to stay with an even predetermined pace which would allow him to catch the leaders late in the race. Raced about once a week. Coached by Albert Hill.

# A SELECTION OF HAL HIGDON SKETCHES FROM THE FIRST EDITION

Rudolph Harbig

Gunder Hagg

John Landy

Herb Elliott

Tom Courtney

Joe Binks

**Fred Wilt**

Fred Wilt was born December 14, 1920 in Pendleton, Indiana. During his running career he was a member of two U.S. Olympic teams (1948 and 1952), set five national records at distances from 2 miles to 10,000 meters, and won ten national championships at distances including one mile, two miles, 5,000m., 10,000m., and cross country. He set a world indoor two-mile record in 1952. Wilt won the AAU's prestigious Sullivan Award in 1950. His citation read, in part: "Holding a responsible position with the FBI, it involved great personal sacrifice for him to keep active in athletics. Obliged to train on a catch-as-catch can basis, early in the morning and late at night, he nevertheless raced gallantly against the strongest available competition on every possible occasion. His sportsmanship was conspicuous in victory and defeat. He made an exhaustive study of training methods and running form employed by the leading European distance specialists and unselfishly made available to the coaches and other competitors the results of his research and experience, thus helping to improve the general standard of distance running here."

Since his retirement from active competition, Fred has continued to serve both the FBI and his sport. He has coached on the high school level in South Carolina and has served on the coaching staffs at the University of Tennessee and Indiana University. Since 1960, he has been editor of the noted periodical, TRACK TECHNIQUE. He has also authored or edited a number of books, including HOW THEY TRAIN, RUN RUN RUN, MECHANICS WITHOUT TEARS, MOTIVATION AND COACHING PSYCHOLOGY (with Ken Bosen), ILLUSTRATED GUIDE TO OLYMPIC TRACK AND FIELD TECHNIQUES (with Tom Ecker), INTERNATIONAL TRACK AND FIELD COACHING ENCYCLOPEDIA (with Tom Ecker), and THE JUMPS: CONTEMPORARY THEORY, TECHNIQUE AND TRAINING.

# BOOKS

## FROM TRACK & FIELD NEWS

**RUNNERS AND RACES: 1500m./Mile,** Cordner Nelson and Roberto Quercetani. This great book is a history of the mile and its metric counterpart, the 1500 meters. Traces all the famous performers and their crucial races: Nurmi, Cunningham, Bannister, Elliott, Snell, Ryun, Keino, et al. Well illustrated. 333pp. Hard cover. 1973. **$6.50**

**KIPCHOGE OF KENYA.** Francis Noronha. Terrific biography of Kip Keino. Good photos and info on Kip. 1970. **$2.50**

**JIM RYUN STORY.** Cordner Nelson's account of the life & career of America's No. 1 track hero, complemented by almost 200 photos by Rich Clarkson. 272pp. 1967. **$5.95**

**FIRST FOUR MINUTES.** Roger Bannister's stirring autobiography: the great account of the 4-min. breakthrough in the mile—perhaps the most famous occurrence in track history. Illustrated. Hard cover. **$3.00**

**THE COMPLETE MIDDLE DISTANCE RUNNER,** Wilson, Horwill, and Watts. Sections on principles of training, strength training, coaching, physiology of exercise, diet, tactics, etc. Good book for coach and runner. Illus. 129pp. **$4.95**

**COMPUTERIZED RUNNING TRAINING PROGRAMS,** Gardner & Purdy. Thousands of computer-generated workouts take the guesswork out of training. Geared to the individual of every ability, every distance. **$4.50**

**LEARNING TO RUN.** Olympian Mal Whitfield aims his book at the younger reader and discusses elements of warm-up, body balance, the mechanics of starting and running, etc. Many valuable tips. 131pp. Well illustrated. **$3.00**

**HIGH SCHOOL RUNNERS & Their Training Programs,** Joe McNeff. "How They Train" for the h.s. runner & coach. Workout programs of over 100 prep aces, including Ryun, Dave Morton, etc., 440-10 miles. 1968. Illus. Soft Cover. **$3.00,** Hard Cover **$5.00**

**RUN RUN RUN,** Fred Wilt. Most useful book ever on running training. All training methods, theory, tactics, warmup and pace, from sprinting thru marathon. 281 packed pages. Paperbound, **$3.50;** Hard cover **$5.50**

**LYDIARD'S RUNNING TRAINING SCHEDULES.** New 2nd ed. 1970. Revised tables & schedules, 880-marathon. **$1.50**

**MIDDLE DISTANCE RUNNING,** Percy Cerutty. One of Cerutty's finest technique works. Hill running, diet, programs for youngsters, schedules, etc. 1964. 195pp. **$6.50**

**MR. CONTROVERSIAL.** The story of Percy Cerutty, the controversial coach of Herb Elliott, John Landy, etc., as told to Graeme Kelly. His methods, philosophy, personality, etc. Illustrated. 1964. 168pp. Hard cover. **$3.95**

**HIGH SCHOOL TRACK—1973.** Reviews & lists for '72, photos, feature articles, etc. Athlete of yr. The bible of high school track. **$1.00**

**TRACK AND FIELD: The Great Ones.** Cordner Nelson focuses on career high points of 13 of history's greatest trackmen: Nurmi, Zatopek, Owens, Elliott, Mathias, etc., with 180 profiles on other major stars of yesterday and today. Illus. 216pp. Hard cover. **$6.50**

**TRACK AND FIELD DYNAMICS,** Tom Ecker. Introduction to the dynamics of body movement in track and field events. Paperbound, **$3.50;** Hard cover **$4.95**

Please add 25¢ per book for postage and handling.

California residents please also add 5% sales tax.

Order from: Track & Field News, Box 296, Los Altos, Calif. 94022